Intellectual Property Law in Fir

Intellectual Property Law in Finland

by
Niklas Bruun

2001

Kluwer Law International
The Hague • London • Boston

Kauppakaari Oyj
Helsinki

Published by Kluwer Law International
P.O. Box 85889
2508 CN The Hague, The Netherlands

Sold and Distributed in North, Central and South America by:
Kluwer Law International
657 Massachusetts Avenue
Cambridge, MA 02139, USA

Sold and distributed in Finland by:
Kauppakaari Oyj
Finnish Lawyers' Publishing
Uudenmaankatu 4–6 A
FIN – 00120 Helsinki, Finland

Sold and Distributed in all other countries by:
Kluwer Law International
Distribution Centre
P.O. Box 322
3300 AH Dordrecht, The Netherlands

Library of Congress Cataloging-in-Publication Data

Printed on acid-free paper

Cover design: The Bears Communications

ISBN 90-411-1544-7 (Kluwer)
ISBN 952-14-0419-0 (Kauppakaari Oyj)

© 2001 Kluwer Law International

Kluwer Law International incorporates the publishing programmes of Graham & Trotman Ltd, Kluwer Law and Taxation Publishers and Martinus Nijhoff Publishers

This publication is protected by international copyright law.
All rights reserved. No part of this publication may be reproduced, stored in a retrieval system, or transmitted in any form or by any means, electronic, mechanical, photocopying, recording or otherwise, without the prior permission of the publisher.

The Author

Niklas Bruun was born on 23 July 1950 in Helsinki. He studied law at the University of Helsinki, graduating in 1972. He continued with postgraduate studies at Helsinki and defended his doctoral thesis in labour law in 1979. He held different positions at the University of Helsinki until he was appointed professor of Commercial Law at Hanken, the Swedish School of Economics and Business Administration in Helsinki from 1986. Since then he has held that professorship, although he was on a leave of absence during the years 1993–1996, being a guest professor in Stockholm, Sweden. He has been chairman, member or secretary of several Government commissions, particularly on Intellectual Property Legislation and Labour Law.

Professor Bruun is the author of several books and a number of articles mainly on Labour Law and Intellectual Property Law. He has been a member of the editorial board of the Nordic Intellectual Property Law Review since 1988. He has been the Chair of the Finnish Society for Industrial Property Law since 1996 and the Chair of the Finnish Copyright Council since 1997. He is also a Member of the board of the Finnish group of the AIPPI (since 1990).

The Author

Table of Contents

The Author	3
Abbreviations	11
Preface	13
General Introduction	15
§1. GENERAL BACKGROUND	15
I. Geography	15
II. Cultural Composition	15
III. Political System	16
IV. Population Statistics	16
§2. HISTORICAL BACKGROUND	18
Select Bibliography	19
Chapter 1. Copyright and Neighbouring Rights	21
§1. SOURCES – LEGISLATION	21
§2. SUBJECT MATTER OF PROTECTION	23
I. Different Categories of Protected Works	23
II. Works Excluded from Protection	26
III. Special Categories of Works	27
A. Computer Software	27
B. Databases	28
§3. CONDITIONS OF PROTECTION	28

Table of Contents

I. Formal Requirements	28
II. Substantive Requirements	29
§4. Ownership	31
I. The Author (Initial Authorship)	31
II. Joint Works/Works Created by Several Persons	32
III. Works Made for Hire	33
§5. Transfer	35
I. Assignment of Copyright	35
II. Licences	36
§6. Scope of Exclusive Rights	40
I. Moral Rights	40
II. Exploitation Rights	42
A. Reproduction Rights	42
B. Performing Rights	44
C. Adaptation Rights	45
D. Translation Rights	46
E. Other Rights	46
1. Droit de Suite	46
2. Public Lending Right	47
3. Others	47
§7. Limitation to or Exemptions from the Scope of Copyright Protection	48
§8. Duration of Protection	54
§9. Neighbouring Rights	56
§10. Infringement and Remedies	60
§11. Overlapping and Relation to Other Intellectual Property Laws	61

Chapter 2. Patents   63

§1. Sources – Legislation	63

Table of Contents

§2. PATENTABLE SUBJECT MATTER	65
§3. CONDITIONS OF PATENTABILITY	68
§4. FORMALITIES (PROCEDURES FOR ISSUING AND OBTAINING PATENT PROTECTION)	72
§5. OWNERSHIP AND TRANSFER (ASSIGNMENT – LICENCES)	77
§6. SCOPE OF EXCLUSIVE RIGHTS	80
§7. LIMITATIONS AND EXCEPTIONS TO THE SCOPE OF PATENT PROTECTION – COMPULSORY LICENCES	83
§8. DURATION OF PROTECTION – MAINTENANCE AND TERMINATION OF PATENT PROTECTION	87
§9. INFRINGEMENT AND REMEDIES	91
§10. OVERLAPPING AND RELATION TO OTHER INTELLECTUAL PROPERTY LAWS	93

Chapter 3. Utility Models — 95

§1. SOURCES – LEGISLATION	95
§2. THE PROTECTION OF UTILITY MODELS	95

Chapter 4. Trademarks — 98

§1. SOURCES – LEGISLATION	98
§2. SUBJECT MATTER OF PROTECTION	100
I. Signs which may Serve as Trademarks	100
II. Various Categories of Marks	101
§3. CONDITIONS OF PROTECTION	104
§4. FORMALITIES (PROCEDURE FOR ACQUIRING PROTECTION, ESTABLISHING AND MAINTAINING TRADEMARKS)	111
§5. OWNERSHIP AND TRANSFER (ASSIGNMENT – LICENCES)	114
§6. SCOPE OF EXCLUSIVE RIGHTS	115

Table of Contents

§7. LIMITATION OF THE SCOPE OF TRADEMARK PROTECTION	119
§8. USE REQUIREMENTS	122
§9. DURATION OF PROTECTION – RENEWAL – TERMINATION	123
§10. INFRINGEMENT AND REMEDIES	125
§11. OVERLAPPING AND RELATION TO OTHER INTELLECTUAL PROPERTY LAWS	127

Chapter 5. Trade Names — 130

§1. SOURCES – LEGISLATION	130
§2. THE PROTECTION OF TRADE NAMES	131

Chapter 6. Industrial Design — 135

§1. SOURCES – LEGISLATION	135
§2. SUBJECT MATTER OF PROTECTION	136
§3. CONDITIONS FOR PROTECTION	136
§4. FORMALITIES (PROCEDURE FOR GRANTING AND ACQUIRING PROTECTION)	138
§5. OWNERSHIP AND TRANSFER (ASSIGNMENT – LICENCES)	139
§6. SCOPE OF EXCLUSIVE RIGHTS	139
§7. LIMITATIONS ON THE SCOPE OF PROTECTION	140
§8. DURATION OF PROTECTION	140
§9. INFRINGEMENT AND REMEDIES	141
§10. OVERLAPPING AND RELATION TO OTHER INTELLECTUAL PROPERTY LAWS	141

Chapter 7. Plant Variety Protection — 142

§1. SOURCES – LEGISLATION	142
§2. SUBJECT MATTER OF PROTECTION	144
§3. CONDITIONS OF PROTECTION	145

Table of Contents

§4. Formalities (Procedure for Granting and Acquiring Protection) — 145

§5. Ownership and Transfer (Assignment – Licences) — 147

§6. Scope of Exclusive Rights — 148

§7. Limitations on the Scope of Protection — 148

§8. Duration of Protection — 149

§9. Infringement and Remedies — 150

§10. Overlapping and Relation to Other Intellectual Property Laws — 151

Chapter 8. Chip Protection — 152

§1. Sources – Legislation — 152

§2. Subject Matter of Protection — 153

§3. Conditions of Protection — 153

§4. Formalities (Procedures for Grant and Obtaining Protection) — 154

§5. Ownership and Transfer (Assignment – Licences) — 155

§6. Scope of Exclusive Rights — 156

§7. Limitations of the Scope of Protection — 156

§8. Duration of Protection — 157

§9. Infringement and Remedies — 158

§10. Overlapping and Relation to Other Intellectual Property Laws — 159

Chapter 9. Trade Secrets/Confidential Information — 160

§1. Sources – Legislation — 160

§2. The Protection of Trade Secrets/Confidential Information — 160

Index — 165

Table of Contents

Abbreviations

AIPPI	Association Internationale pour la Protection de la Propriété Industrielle (International Association for the Protection of Industrial Property)
CPC	Community Patent Convention
CPVR	Community Plant Variety Right
DL	Defensor Legis
EEA	The European Economic Area
ECJ	European Court of Justice
EPC	European Patent Convention
EPO	European Patent Organisation
EU	European Union
GATT	General Agreement on Tariffs and Trade
GRUR	Gewerblicher Rechtsschutz und Urheberrecht
KM	Komiteamietintö (Committee Report)
KTM	Kauppa- ja teollisuusministeriö; Ministry of Trade and Industry
LM	Lakimies
NBPR	National Board of Patents and Registration
NIR	Nordiskt immateriellt rättsskydd (Nordic Intellectual Property Law Review)
NORD	København: Nordisk Ministerråd
NU	Nordisk utredningsserie, joint committee report of the Nordic countries
OJ	Official Journal of the European Communities
PCT	The Patent Co-operation Treaty
SAC	Supreme Administrative Court
SC	Supreme Court
SOU	Statens offentliga utredningar; Swedish Committee Reports
TRIPS	Agreement on Trade Related Aspects of Intellectual Property Rights
UPOV	International Convention for the Protection of New Varieties of Plants
WIPO	World Intellectual Property Organisation (French abbr. OMPI)

Abbreviations

Preface

There has been very little written in English on general Finnish intellectual property law, although some useful specialist reports have been submitted to international organisations such as the WIPO, AIPPI, the EU, etc. A few specialised monographs have also appeared recently. This general presentation is therefore the first of its kind in English.

The preparation of this monograph could not have been possible without the expert assistance of many people. Claes von Heiroth LL M wrote the first draft of several chapters, Mia Bengts LL M and Laura Wennonen LL M were also very helpful in many respects. Experts in various fields, patent attorney Pia Hjelt, Deputy Director General Sirkka-Liisa Lahtinen of the National Board of Patents and Registration of Finland and Jukka Palm LL.Lic. have supplied useful comments on individual chapters. Responsibility for the final text lies entirely with the author, although last but not least Daryl Taylor BA, BSc, partly assisted by Finn Nielsen Ph.D., has done a tremendous job in transforming the manuscript into decent English. My warm thanks to all these persons and others who, in one way or another, have made this work possible.

Helsinki, 9 May 1998

Niklas Bruun

Preface

General Introduction

§1. General Background

I. Geography

1. Finland is one of the five Nordic countries. It lies between Sweden and Russia and stretches from the Baltic Sea to the Norwegian border near the Arctic Ocean. The country covers 305,475 square kilometres, making it the fifth largest country in Europe. The climate is usually severe with snow in the winter and temperatures dropping as low as $-30°C$.

2. Finland is famous for its many lakes and other inland waters, and is therefore often referred to as 'the land of 1000 lakes'. In the northern parts of Finland live the Sami; an indigenous people of the Fenno-Scandinavian North and the Russian North-West. The Åland Islands in the South-West of the country are also under Finnish sovereignty, enjoying a special constitutional autonomy granted by international agreement in 1921.

II. Cultural Composition

3. Culturally, Finland is part of Scandinavia. There are two national languages: Finnish and Swedish. The Swedish speaking minority comprises 6 per cent of the population. Swedish is mainly spoken along the western coastline. Finnish is not an Indo-European language and is not understood in the other Scandinavian countries.

4. Finnish industry has traditionally centred around forestry and the paper industry. Pulp, paper and a variety of sawn goods are made for export. The engineering industry is also an important field with links to the paper mills. The electronics industry has increased rapidly in recent years and Nokia is the Finnish leader in patent application statistics.

5. Finland became a member of the European Union in 1995 following a referendum and, since the early 1980s, has gradually moved towards a new openness. Foreign investors have found their way to Finland and it is no longer unusual for a Finnish company to have foreign subsidiaries.

III. Political System

6. Finland was an integral part of Sweden between 1150 and 1809, and so Finland has strong cultural ties to Swedish intellectual life. Finland became an autonomous Grand Duchy within the Russian Empire in 1809 but retained its own laws and constitution from the Swedish era, while the Emperor of Russia enjoyed the title of Grand Duke of Finland. Finland became an independent republic in 1917. Soon after this, social and political controversies escalated into a civil war between the 'Whites' and the 'Reds' (socialists), which ended with the victory of the former.

7. The Constitution Act of 1919 replaced the old Swedish constitution. It introduced the doctrine of tripartite division of powers and clearly determines the three branches of the State, i.e. the legislature, the executive and the judiciary. The three powers were intended to be independent of each other but the separation of powers has become somewhat blurred by the strong position of the executive in relation to the legislature.

8. Legislative power is vested in Parliament and the President. A unicameral Parliament was adopted as long ago as 1906. Parliament is elected for a term of four years. Executive power is vested in the President sitting in Cabinet. The Cabinet, however, must enjoy the confidence of Parliament (parliamentarism). The President is elected for a term of six years and may be re-elected. Presidential powers are extensive and the President enjoys a high status due to the strong personalities and long terms of former holders of this office. Judicial power is in the hands of independent tribunals organised into two branches: the general courts and the administrative courts.

9. Following the Second World War some eastern parts of the country were ceded to the Soviet Union, while their Finnish inhabitants were resettled in the remaining parts of the country. A formerly agrarian Finland became a highly industrialised country and soon developed into one of the Scandinavian welfare states. Finland was also an active member of the League of Nations, and has subsequently been involved in the UN and its agencies as well as in other international organisations. The country has conducted a consistent policy of non-alignment.

IV. Population Statistics

10. The population of modern Finland is approximately 5 million. Population growth has been quite rapid from a figure of 1,7 million in 1860. However, the annual growth rate has gradually declined (not counting the post-war boom of the late 1940s) and the average age of the population is now rapidly increasing. Finland has also experienced considerable emigration between the 1880s and the First World War, when approximately 300,000 Finns emigrated to North America. A second emigration wave to Sweden came in 1960–1970, when unemployment

forced people to move. The mortality rates of children and infants have fallen continuously since the 18th century because of a higher standard of living, better hygiene and the development of medical science.

§2. Historical Background

11. The Paris Convention (Convention de Paris pour la protection de la propriété industrielle, 1883) is the most important international convention on intellectual property. Finland ratified the Paris Convention in 1921. Since then Finnish trademark law has been harmonised with it. The Nordic trademark acts are the result of co-operation conducted on a voluntary basis between these countries. The Nordic countries also prepared their patent acts jointly in the 1960s, resulting in a joint committee report.[1] The basic principles of the Nordic patent acts are similar and the differences between them are rather minor.

1   NU 1963: 6.

12. The Berne Convention (Convention de Berne pour la protection des oeuvres littéraires et artistiques, 1886) on copyright was ratified by Finland in 1928. Finland also ratified the Convention Establishing the World Intellectual Property Organisation (WIPO) in May 1970 and the convention became effective in Finland as of 8 September 1970.

13. Intellectual property with the exception of copyright law falls within the administrative domain of the Ministry of Trade and Industry. The ministry is responsible for development and legislation pertaining to these rights. The National Board of Patents and Registration of Trademarks, which was founded in 1942, is an authority subordinate to the Ministry of Trade and Industry. Immediately before the establishment of the Board, patents, trademarks and registration matters were processed by a separate department at the Ministry of Trade and Industry. The Board handles all matters relating to patents, utility models, industrial designs, trade names, trademarks and chip protection. The National Board of Patents and Registration also has a Board of Appeals which is a part of the Patent Office and is thus not entirely independent of the registration authority.

14. The District Court of Helsinki is the sole competent court of first instance in respect of intellectual property disputes concerning industrial design, patents and trademarks in Finland. The court is assisted in these matters by two technical experts who submit their views on the disputes at hand. These experts are appointed by the court.

Selected Bibliography

IN FINNISH OR NORDIC LANGUAGES:

Aro, P.-L., '*Ennakkokäyttöoikeus patentinhaltijan yksinoikeuden rajoituksena*' [The Right of Prior Use as a Limitation on the Exclusive Rights of a Patent Holder], Suomalainen lakimiesyhdistys, Vammala 1972;
Bruun, N., Uppfinnarrätt i auställningsfoihällande (or Employee Inventions), Iyväskylä 1982;
Castrén, M., '*EU-Suomen markkinaoikeus*' [Market Law in EU-Finland], Helsinki 1997;
Castrén, M., '*Toiminimi*' [Trade Name], Finnish Lawyers' Publishing Company, Mikkeli 1984;
Drockila, L., '*Tavaramerkkien sekoitettavuudesta ja harhaanjohtavuudesta*' [The Confusing Similarity and Misleading Character of Trademarks], Lakimiesliiton kustannus, Helsinki 1986;
Godenhielm, B., '*Patentskyddets omfattning*' [On the Scope of Patent Protection], Juristförbundets förlag, Helsinki 1994;
Godenhielm, B., '*Om ekvivalens och annat gott*' [On Equivalence], Söderström & Co Förlag, Ekenäs 1990;
Godenhielm, B., '*Uppsatser i immaterialaätt*' [Essays on Intellectual Property], Norstedt & Söners Förlag, Stockholm 1983;
Haarmann, P.-L., '*Immateriaalioikeuden oppikirja*' [A Textbook of Intellectual Property Rights] 2nd ed., Lakimiesliiton kustannus, Helsinki 1994;
Haarmann, P.-L., '*Tekijänoikeus, lähioikeudet ja oikeus valokuvaan*' [Copyright, Neighbouring Rights and the Right to a Photographic Image], Finnish Lawyers' Publishing Company, Helsinki 1992;
Tiili, V. & Aro, P.-L., '*Yrityksen tavaramerkki- ja mallisuojaopas*' [An Enterprise's Guide to Trademarks and Registration of Designs] 1st ed., Kauppalehti Business Books, Jyväskylä 1986.

IN ENGLISH:

Aro, P.-L., 'A Finnish Case on Compulsory Licence' in NIR No. 1, 1985, pp. 91–98;
Bruun, N., 'The Role of the Patent System in the Protection of Intellectual Property' in NIR No. 2, 1992, pp. 205–216;
Bruun, N., 'Joint Inventors/Joint Patentees' in NIR No. 4, 1993, pp. 590–600;

Selected Bibliography

Castrén, M., 'The Patentability of Biotechnical Inventions in Finland' in NIR No. 1, 1996, pp. 9–21;

Castrén, M. & Kolster, B., 'Non-confusing Use of Another's Trademark' in AIPPI Q 95 No. 7, 1988, pp. 134–146;

Godenhielm, B., *'Employee Inventions'*, Ch. 7 in Ulmer, E., Copyright and Industrial Copyright, Vol. XIV of International Encyclopedia of Comparative Law (J.C.B. Mohr, Tübingen);

Hilli, R., *'Trade Marks'*, Ch. 6 in Metaxas-Maranghidis, Intellectual Property Laws of Europe (Chansery Law Publishing, Chichester 1995);

Hilli, R. *et al.*, 'Enforcement of Intellectual Property Rights – Procedure and Sanctions' in AIPPI Q 134A No. 4, 1996, pp. 175–180;

Kolster, B. *et al.*, 'Trademarks: Conflicts with Prior Rights' in AIPPI Q 104 No. 4, 1991, pp. 65–68;

Nordman, E. *et al.*, 'Enforcement of Intellectual Property Rights – Procedure and Sanctions' in AIPPI Q 134B No. 5, 1996, pp. 155–174;

Pfanner, K., 'Compulsory Licensing of Patents; survey and recent trends' in NIR No. 1, 1985, pp. 1–29;

Rissanen, K., 'Protection of Collective and Certification Marks' in AIPPI Q 72 No. 1, 1982, pp. 38–41;

Salokannel, M., *'Ownership of Rights in Audiovisual Productions'*, Kluwer Law International, The Hague 1997.

Tommila, M. *et al.*, 'Trademark Licensing and Franchising' in AIPPI Q 116 No. 4, 1993, pp. 93–98;

Tommila, M. *et al.*, 'House Marks' in AIPPI Q 107 No. 7, 1991, pp. 46–56;

Chapter 1. Copyright and Neighbouring Rights

§1. SOURCES – LEGISLATION

Bibliography in Finnish or Nordic languages:
Bruun, N., 'Otillåten, tillåten och överlåten avbildning i upphovsrätten' [Forbidden, Permitted and Assigned Duplication in Copyright Law], in *'Festskrift til Birger Stuevold Lassen'*, Universitetsforlaget, Oslo 1997;
Godenhielm, B., *'Uppsatser i immaterialrätt'* [Essays in Intellectual Property Law], Norstedt & Söners Förlag, Stockholm 1983;
Haarmann, P.-L., *'Immateriaalioikeuden oppikirja'* [A Textbook of Intellectual Property Law] 2nd ed., Finnish Lawyers' Publishing Company, Helsinki 1994;
Haarmann, P.-L., *'Tekijänoikeus, lähioikeudet ja oikeus valokuvaan'* [Copyright, Neighbouring Rights and the Right to a Photographic Image], Finnish Lawyers' Publishing Company, Helsinki 1992;
Koktvedgaard, M. & Levin, M., *'Lärobok i immaterialrätt'* [A Textbook of Intellectual Property Law], Norstedts Juridik, Stockholm 1997;
Oesch, R., *'Vuoden 1995 tekijänoikeusuudistuksen pääkohtia'* [Some Principal Points in the 1995 Reform of Copyright Law], in DL, Nos. 11–12, 1995, pp. 886–900;
Olsson, H., *'Upphovsrättslagstiftningen'* [Copyright Legislation], Norstedts Juridik, Stockholm 1996.

Bibliography in English:
Cornish, W.R., *'Intellectual Property'*, 3rd ed., Sweet & Maxwell, London 1996;
Hilli, R., 'Copyright', Ch. 6.1 in Metaxas-Maranghidis, *'Intellectual Property Laws of Europe'* (Chansery Law Publishing, Chichester 1995), pp. 125–130;
Rosen, J., 'Moral Right in Swedish Copyright Law' in NIR No. 3, 1993;
Salokannel, M., *'Ownership of Rights in Audiovisual Productions'*, Kluwer Law International, The Hague 1997.

Official documents:
Government Bill 1992/211;
Government Bill 1993/94;
Government Bill 1994/287;
Government Bill 1995/8;
Government Bill 1995/42;
Government Bill 1996/185;
Government Bill 1997/43;
Swedish Committee Report SOU 1956:25.

15. The current Copyright Act[1] entered into force on 1 September 1961 as a result of Nordic co-operation during the 1940s to 1960s aimed at harmonising Nordic copyright legislation. Even though each country had national committees making reports during the preparation work, the legislations of the different coun-

tries were harmonised to a large extent. Thus, the Swedish committee report, which is an extensive study and review of copyright legislation, may still also be useful in interpreting the provisions of the Finnish Copyright Act in specific cases.[2]

1. Copyright Act, No. 404 of 8 July 1961 (as last amended by Act No. 365 of 25 April 1997).
2. SOU 1956:25.

16. The Copyright Act has been amended several times since 1961. Even though there have been joint Nordic preparation committees, the amendments have not always been harmonised. Furthermore, in Denmark the copyright legislation has been comprehensively revised. Thus, the Nordic copyright laws are nowadays no longer as well harmonised as they used to be.

17. The Copyright Act was harmonised with community law in connection with Finnish membership of the European Union.[1] In 1995 the Act was extensively amended in order to harmonise it with new community law,[2] while at the same time provisions on protection for photographs were brought into the Copyright Act[3] and a system of remuneration to the artist for the resale of fine art was introduced. The amendment also introduced many minor and technical changes.[4]

1. Council Directive of 14 May 1991 on the legal protection of computer programs (91/250/EEC), Council Directive of 19 November 1992 on rental right and lending right and on certain rights related to copyright in the field of intellectual property (92/100/EEC), Council Directive of 27 September 1993 on the co-ordination of certain rules concerning copyright and rights related to copyright applicable to satellite broadcasting and cable retransmission (93/83/ EEC), Council Directive of 29 October 1993 harmonising the term of protection of copyright and certain related rights (93/98/EEC), Directive of the European Parliament and of the Council of 11 March 1996 on the legal protection of databases (96/9/EC); Proposal for a European Parliament and Council Directive on the resale right for the benefit of the author of an original work of art (96/C 178/05) COM (96) 97 final 96/085 (COD).
2. Council Directive 92/100/EEC on rental and lending rights and on certain rights related to copyright in the field of intellectual property, Council Directive 93/83/EEC on the co-ordination of certain rules concerning copyright and rights related to copyright applicable to satellite broadcasting and cable transmissions.
3. The old Act on the Protection of Photographs was correspondingly repealed.
4. Act No. 446 of 34 March 1995.

18. Finland ratified the 1886 Berne Convention as long ago as 1928, the 1952 Universal Copyright Convention in 1963, the 1961 Rome Convention in 1983 and the 1971 Geneva Convention in 1973. Finland is also bound by the TRIPS Agreement.[1] Thus, Finnish legislation on copyright and neighbouring rights is harmonised to a large extent with international conventions.

1. Agreement on Trade-Related Aspects of Intellectual Property Rights (1994).

19. Besides the Copyright Act and Copyright Decree,[1] the judgments of the Supreme Court (SC) and the Court of Appeal[2] constitute important sources of law. In several areas there is, however, rather little case law. The advisory opinions of the Copyright Council[3] on the interpretation of the Copyright Act in individual cases are therefore also important, even though these are not legally binding. These advisory opinions are provided free of charge. Furthermore, cases and material from the other Nordic countries may also be used to some extent, especially the Swedish committee report SOU 1956:25 referred to above. As Finland is endeavouring to meet the requirements imposed by international conventions, guidelines for interpretation may also be found in the conventions and other international material.[4]

1. Decree No. 574 of 21 April 1995.
2. The Court of Appeal of Helsinki and the Court of Appeal of Turku are the most important.
3. The Copyright Council (*Tekijänoikeusneuvosto* in Finnish) issues advisory opinions on matters of copyright. Both private individuals, corporations and public authorities such as courts of law, may request an opinion. Since the number of Supreme Court and Court of Appeal decisions is limited, the opinions of the Copyright Council are of considerable practical importance in interpreting the law.
4. P.-L. Haarmann (1992) p. 25.

§2. Subject Matter of Protection

I. Different Categories of Protected Works

20. The Copyright Act provides protection for a wide range of different works. The two main groups subject to copyright protection are literary and artistic works. Neighbouring rights are protected in Chapter 5 of the Act. These are further divided into several categories.

21. Section 1 of the Copyright Act provides that literary and artistic works may be protected by copyright. The expression 'literary and artistic works' is to be interpreted extensively. However, it excludes the protection of, for example, inventions, ideas, games, scientific theories, methods and processes.

22. Literary works are imaginary, scientific and descriptive literature in written or spoken form, and may also include, for example, improvised speeches, databases and catalogues, where these satisfy the requirements for classification as works. Even private letters or interviews are subject to copyright.[1] Section 1, paragraph 2 provides that maps and other descriptive drawings as well as computer programs are also to be considered as literary works.

1. The right may belong to the interviewer, to the interviewee or to both, depending on the circumstances (H. Olsson p. 37).

23. All kinds of novels, poems and scientific literature are regarded as literary works. Descriptive literature, such as manuals, brochures,[1] cookery-books, etc., usually also meets the requirements. Receipts themselves, however, do not normally enjoy protection. Articles in magazines and newspapers are nowadays regarded as works. Only news in brief, announcements and notices fall outside of the scope of protection. In interviews, the owner of the copyright is the writer, not the interviewee.[2] The conditions for letters to qualify for protection used to be high but nowadays these may acquire protection more easily.[3] Maps, drawings, etc. are protected by Section 1, paragraph 2, and the requirements for their originality and creativity are lower than for other works.[4] Contracts or terms of contract enjoy protection only rarely.[5]

1. *See*, for example, *Copyright Council 1986:2 (Ski-info)*.
2. In some circumstances, however, a joint ownership might arise.
3. The confidentiality of correspondence may have bearing on this, however.
4. However, in *SC 1988:4* the Court held that drawings of a building may acquire protection even though the building itself is not protected. However, in the actual case cited, the drawings also lacked originality and thus were not protected.
5. M. Koktvedgaard & M. Levin p. 75.

24. *Artistic works* are all other kinds of work, and Section 1 gives a list of examples of them. According to the list, an artistic work may be 'a musical or dramatic work, a cinematographic work, a photographic work or other work of fine art, a product of architecture, artistic handicraft, industrial art, or may be expressed in some other manner'. It should be noted that this list in no way excludes other kinds of works from protection. Moreover, the works need not include any 'artistic' elements, but, for example, products of scientific research and technical drawings may also acquire protection.

25. The following decisions of the courts and of the Copyright Council illustrate what kinds of work may or may not acquire copyright protection.

SC 1988:52
The Supreme Court held that a television commentary on a football match which met the requirement of originality was protected by copyright.
Court of Appeal of Helsinki decision of 25 November 1971
The interior of a private apartment designed by an interior designer was not held to be a work of art of the kind referred to in the Copyright Act.
Copyright Council 1986:3
A system for information processing was not such as to be regarded as a literary or artistic work. However, a computer program that was a part of the system could acquire protection.
Copyright Council 1986:8
A manuscript of a motion picture and the motion picture based on a script was protected by copyright. A character created in the script and the motion picture had been used separately from the said works. Such use was held to be the use of an idea from the works and the character was not protected by copyright.

26. *Works of pictorial art.* Works of pictorial art easily acquire protection. Advertisements may also be protected as works of pictorial art, in which case they must meet the normal requirements for works. The layouts of advertisements do not normally obtain protection.

27. *Products of architecture.* Not only are buildings considered to be products of architecture, but also bridges, ships, landscape architecture and so on. Furthermore, both the structures concerned and the drawings for them are considered to be products of architecture.[1] Thus, the drawings may be protected both as products of architecture and as literary works.[2] Copyright prohibits both the copying of the drawings and the construction of a building similar to that depicted in the drawings. Where, however, descriptive drawings describe something other than a work enjoy-

ing copyright protection, for example a technical machine, only the drawings are protected.

1. P.-L. Haarmann (1992) p. 69.
2. Where the building (etc.) is not considered to be a product of architecture, the drawings are protected only as literary works.

28. Artistic handicrafts and industrial arts. Artistic handicrafts and industrial arts include a very wide range of products. For example jewellery, furniture, light fittings, shag rugs, tools, utensils and many other kinds of applied arts are included in these categories.

SC 1962 II 60 (Bracelet)
The Supreme Court held that a bracelet designed by an artist was to be regarded as an artistic work and was thus protected.
SC 1980 II 3 (Jewellery and clasps)
The Supreme Court held that the jewellery concerned was to be regarded as an artistic work, whereas the clasps were not.

29. Photographic works and pictures. Since the 1995 amendments, photographic works have been protected by copyright pursuant to Section 1, whereas photographic pictures are protected by Section 49a. The protection of photographic pictures is a neighbouring right which is weaker than copyright. Pictures are regarded as photographic works when they meet the requirements of originality and creativity. These should be assessed on similar grounds as in the case of other works of pictorial art.[1] However, it will not be easy to draw a distinction in practice between photographic works and pictures.

1. Government Bill 1994/287 p. 54.

30. It should be noted that Sections 1 and 49a protect only the picture and that the subject falls outside of the protection. Therefore, there may be many almost identical pictures of the same subject with all of them enjoying protection. However, where the subject is a protected work, it may be an infringement to take a picture of it.

SC 1994:99 (Hiltunen v. Lehtikuva, Topitörmä, Veho)[1]
An advertisement for automobiles included a photograph in which two sculptures were dominating. The consent of the copyright holder of the photograph for the use thereof did not include the consent of the sculptor for the use of the sculptures shown in the advertisement.

1. There is a commentary on this case by N. Bruun in Festskrift til Birger Stuevold Lassen.

31. Cinematographic works. It is clear that traditional cinematographic works, including films, documentaries, short films and animations, are protected as such. The situation becomes less clear concerning the wide range of various television programs. However, the concept of 'cinematographic work' has broadened considerably in recent years and it has been considered that in practice the majority of television programs are protected. Even if a cinematographic work has not acquired protection, the individual pictures of a cinematographic work may be protected as photographs pursuant to Section 49a.[1] As has already been noted, computer games have not been regarded as cinematographic works in Finland, but as computer programs. This view has been criticised and differs from the situation in some other countries.[2]

1. P.-L. Haarmann (1992) p. 197.
2. M. Salokannel pp. 77*ff*.

32. Audio-visual works. In Finland there are no special provisions on audio-visual works. Therefore, the general rules on copyright are applied to them including, in particular, the rules on cinematographic works and compilation works.

33. Title, pseudonym and signature. Section 51 provides that a work may not be made available to the public under any title, pseudonym or signature which is such that the work or its author may easily be confused with a previously disseminated work or with its author. Thus without the authors consent it is not permitted to give a novel the same name as, for example, a motion picture. A title need not be 'original and creative' in order to acquire such protection. However, a simple title such as 'A Textbook of Intellectual Property' cannot be regarded as leading to confusion. In rare cases the title itself may be protected by copyright where it has originality and creativity.[1]

1. P.-L. Haarmann (1994) p. 59.

34. Compilation works. Section 5 provides that a person who, by combining works or parts of works, creates a compilation work, shall have copyright thereto. For example multimedia works for computers may be regarded as compilation works.

35. Original and secondary works. Works may also be divided into original and secondary works. Where an original work is translated or adapted, or where many works have been combined, a secondary work is created. The translator or adapter acquires copyright to the secondary work, but this latter copyright is limited by the copyright to the original work (Sects. 4 and 5). Examples of secondary works include a translated novel, a filmed novel, a newspaper, an encyclopaedia and a movie. The owner of secondary rights may exercise these rights only with the consent of the owner of the rights to the original work and thus the rights to the original work are in no way limited by the secondary rights. It should be noted that the Copyright Act protects only translations (etc.) of *works*. Therefore, where news, catalogues, or other kind of products not enjoying protection are translated (etc.), then the translation is not protected. The original copyright need not, however, be still in force. Thus a translation of, for example, a classic novel, the copyright of which has expired, is nevertheless protected.

II. Works Excluded from Protection

36. Public authorities. In Finland there is no equivalent to *crown copyright* or the like. Section 9 provides that there is no copyright to Acts and Decrees of statute, or to the ordinances [decisions] and declarations of public authorities and other public bodies. Even though there can be no copyright in Acts and Decrees, it should be noted that where such Acts and Decrees have been collected and combined into a compilation work, e.g. the 'Finnish Law' collection,[1] then the author of such a work has copyright thereto.

1. A well-known standard collection of Statutes and case law used by lawyers in Finland.

37. The expression 'public authorities and other public bodies' is to be understood extensively. It includes all authorities of the government, the municipalities and the established churches, as well as other autonomous bodies of the administration. The expression 'decrees [decisions] and declarations' refers to written, but not oral decisions, declarations, reports, proposals and statements. However, commentaries on Acts, handbooks, maps and catalogues are not excluded from this protection. Section 25c provides that oral or written statements in a public presentation or before an authority or at public meetings concerning matters of public interest may be used without the author's consent.

38. *Integrated circuits.* [microprocessor, design circuit] The Act on the Exclusive Right to the Layout-Design (Topography) of an Integrated Circuit[1] provides protection for integrated circuits. These are excluded from copyright protection (Sect. 10, para. 2 of the Copyright Act). The Act on integrated circuits entered into force on 16 January 1991. If an integrated circuit was designed before that date, then it might have acquired copyright protection provided that it meets the requirements for a work. The protection of integrated circuits is considered in Chapter 8 on chip protection.

1. Act No. 32 of 11 January 1991.

III. Special Categories of Works

A. Computer Software

39. In 1991 Section 1, paragraph 2 was amended to include a provision that computer programs are to be deemed literary works.[1] Therefore, where a computer program reaches the level of a work, it is protected by copyright in the same way as any other work. As for other works, copyright does not protect ideas or general principles as such but only the original and creative form of manifestation of the ideas and principles. The program is protected regardless of the form of manifestation. Thus, it is not relevant whether it is expressed in object code or source code, nor is it relevant on what physical medium the program is stored. It might be noted that a computer game is protected as a compilation work consisting of the program itself as a literary program, the pictures as works of art and the sound as a musical work.[2]

1. In practice computer programs had also been regarded as literary works before the provision was enacted.
2. P.-L. Haarmann (1992) p. 66.

40. There are some special provisions concerning copying for private use, public lending and certain kinds of reproduction applicable to computer programs. These will be considered later. The Copyright Act was harmonised with the Directive on legal protection of computer programs in 1993.[1]

  1. Council Directive 91/250/EEC of 14 May 1991 on the legal protection of computer programs.

B. Databases

41. Databases may be protected as literary works, as compilations, or on the basis of the special provisions provided in Section 49 concerning catalogues. Where a database consists of works or parts thereof, it is regarded as a *compilation*, provided that the works concerned are chosen and arranged in a manner displaying creativity and originality. Where the works are chosen according to fixed rules, the database does not enjoy the protection of a compilation. If the database is made up of individual items of information which are not protected separately, and these are organised in a manner displaying creativity and originality, then the database enjoys copyright protection as an independent *work*.

42. However, if a database is considered to be neither a work nor a compilation, i.e. it is not considered to be the result of intellectual creativity, then it may nevertheless enjoy protection as a *database* under a specific provision of Section 49.[1] Section 49 provides that a catalogue, table, programme or other production, in which a large number of information items are compiled may not be reproduced without the consent of the producer. It might be noted that whereas the use of even a part of a database which is protected as a work by copyright is within the scope of exclusive rights, catalogues are protected only against copying.[2] Section 49 has recently been harmonised with the Database Directive.[3]

  1. Protection for catalogues is a neighbouring right.
  2. Government Bill 1987:8 (summary in English) pp. 10*ff*.
  3. Directive of the European Parliament and of the Council of 11 July 1996 on the legal protection of databases (96/9/EC).

§3. Conditions of Protection

I. Formal Requirements

43. The Berne Convention provides that copyright protection is not to be dependent upon any formalities. This principle is also adhered to in Finland and thus there are no formal requirements for obtaining copyright. Even though the copyright sign (©), the name of the copyright holder and the year of publishing are commonly used, they have no legal effect on the protection, since this protection subsists in all works. The sign merely serves as a reminder that the concerned work is protected.[1]

  1. H. Olsson p. 426.

II. Substantive Requirements

44. A production or creation must meet certain substantive requirements in order to acquire copyright protection. The Copyright Act does not explicitly provide these requirements. It only states that '[a] person who has created a literary or artistic work shall have copyright thereto'. However, in the *travaux préparatoires* it was indicated that these words refer to and include the internationally accepted requirements for protected works.[1]

   1. P.-L. Haarmann (1992) p. 52.

45. The requirements of *creativity and originality* are the most important conditions for a production or creation to attain the status of a work. In the *travaux préparatoires* it is stated that a work is the result of original creative expression.[1] Therefore, products that are the result of only mechanical activity, or which result from copying existing works, do not obtain protection.

   1. Committee Report 1990:31 p. 25.

46. When considering originality and creativity, no heed is paid to artistic or aesthetic criteria, nor to any other ethical or moral criteria. Protection does not, therefore, depend on the quality of the work.[1] 'Originality' does not mean that the work has to be original or novel with regard to other works, but merely that the work is the result of the personal creative act of the author and is not copied from another work.[2] This means that objective originality or novelty is not a prerequisite for protection. 'Labour and skill' are, contrary to the state of affairs in some other countries, insignificant for protection in Finland. It does not matter how much labour and skill the author has used in creating the product if the product is not original and creative.[3]

   1. P.-L. Haarmann (1992) p. 55.
   2. W. R. Cornish pp. 334–335.
   3. P.-L. Haarmann (1992) p. 57.

47. It is clear that an author is usually more or less influenced by earlier works. Also, works often derive in some sense from earlier sources. This does not necessarily mean that the new product lacks creativity or originality. This principle is expressed in Section 4, paragraph 2. This provides that if a new and independent work is created in free connection with the earlier one, then the copyright to the new work is not dependent upon copyright to the older work. It is international practice that, for example, parodies, travesties, etc. are considered to be independent works. The following Supreme Court decision illustrates the principle.

SC 1979 II 64 (Painting of a photograph)
A painter had used a photograph as a model for a painting. The Court held that the painting was not a copy of the photograph, but that it was an independent work which had been made using the photograph as a model. The Court referred to Section 4, paragraph 2 and held that the painter had not infringed the rights of the photographer.

48. Section 44a provides an exemption to the requirement of originality and creativity. According to this, anyone who, for the first time, publishes or disseminates a previously unpublished or non-disseminated work is entitled to hold copyright to the work. However, it is required that the unpublished work has been previously protected in Finland and that such protection has expired.

49. What is required of a work to attain 'the status of a work' varies between various categories of works. Whereas the threshold to be considered a work is quite low in traditional areas such as literature, music or art, it can be reasonably high in the case of applied arts, for example. The possibility of acquiring protection for applied art in the form of industrial designs in accordance with the Registered Designs Act[1] may have influenced the possibilities of acquiring copyright protection for the same products.[2] Moreover, if applied arts were to be too easy to protect by copyright, then this could have negative effects on competition.[3]

 1. Act No. 221 of 12 March 1971 as last amended by Act No. 718 of 21 April 1995.
 2. Godenhielm (1983) p. 79.
 3. M. Koktvedgaard & M. Levin p. 79.

50. Literary works. As already mentioned, a high degree of originality and creativity is not required for literary works. There are no requirements as to the length of the work and even the name of a novel, for example, might in some circumstances acquire protection, provided that it has sufficient originality and creativity.[1]

 1. P.-L. Haarmann (1992) p. 60.

Court of Appeal of Helsinki decision of 6 February 1996 (Calendars and forms)
The defendant had published calendars and some forms which resembled the calendars and forms of the plaintiff, and the plaintiff alleged that the defendant had infringed his copyright. However, the Court held that neither the calendars nor the forms showed the degree of originality and creativity required for works to acquire protection. Therefore, the calendars were held to be neither literary nor compilation works and the forms were not held to be literary works. Furthermore, the forms could not be protected as catalogues in the manner provided in Section 49.

51. Works of pictorial art. Generally speaking, the requirements for pictorial art (paintings, drawings, sculptures, photographic works, etc.) to attain the status of a work are not particularly high. One special kind of work consists of advertisements. These may obtain copyright protection where they meet the general conditions for protection.[1] It has been argued that the layout of advertisements could also acquire protection.[2] However, with respect to layouts the requirements for originality and creativity have been made rather high and thus in practice layouts do not normally acquire protection.[3]

 1. *See* the *Court of Appeal of Turku judgment of 27 September 1985.* The Court held that a large outdoor advertisement consisting of a picture and a short text was an artistic work.
 2. However, compare with P.-L. Haarmann (1992) p. 68.
 3. *See* e.g. *Copyright Council 1990:8.*

52. Products of architecture. It is clear that major architectural creations enjoy protection. However, the situation is less clear in respect of smaller standardised houses and practice has varied. Nevertheless, there are at least two cases in which detached houses have been protected.[1] When assessing originality and creativity the courts have regard mainly to the façade, but also to some extent the interiors.[2]

> 1. See *Copyright Council 1987:6* and *Court of Appeal of Eastern-Finland judgment of 24 August 1989.*
> 2. It seems that in the other Nordic countries protection is obtained more readily.

53. Artistic handicrafts and industrial arts. The requirements for artistic handicrafts and industrial arts to acquire protection are generally set at a fairly high level.[1]

> 1. On the other hand, they may be protected as registered designs.

Court of Appeal of Helsinki decision of 29 May 1985 (Light fittings)
The Court held that light fittings did not enjoy copyright protection even though they had been designed by an internationally recognised designer.
Copyright Council 1986:13 (Boat)
It was held that a boat did not meet the requirements of originality and creativity and thus the boat itself was not protected by copyright. The drawings of the boat were protected as literary works.

54. Cinematographic works. Cinematographic works must meet the same general requirements for originality and creativity as other works, i.e. they may be considered as original and independent expressions of the author's personality. It should be noted that neither the technique whereby the work is recorded nor the medium on which it has been fixed is of any significance for protection. Therefore, live television transmissions may also be protected, which is contrary to the situation in, for example, the United States.[1]

> 1. M. Salokannel p. 71.

§4. OWNERSHIP

I. The Author (Initial Authorship)

55. Section 1 provides that a *person* who has created a work shall have copyright thereto. It is a generally accepted principle that the initial ownership to copyright is always held by one or several individuals, i.e. the *author or authors.* Therefore, a body corporate may obtain copyright only by assignment.[1] However, with respect to computer programs and databases created by an employee, Section 40b provides that the rights thereto are automatically transferred to the employer. In the case of cinematographic and other works involving several persons, ownership of rights is usually governed by contractual relationships.

> 1. Note that this rule does not apply to all neighbouring rights.

56. There are no formal requirements on the person of the author. The author may be any *physical person*, regardless of age, responsibility, sanity, etc. However, the author must be a human being, which means that it cannot, for example, be an animal.[1] When works are created by using computers or other machines, these are also regarded as tools and the author is usually the person controlling the tool.[2]

   1. For example in some cases chimpanzees have painted paintings. However, there has been no copyright on those paintings (M. Koktvedgaard & M. Levin p. 71).
   2. Committee Report 1987:8 p. 65.

57. Where a work has been *translated or adapted*, the translator or adapter has the copyright to the work in the new form. This right is, however, subject to the copyright to the original work (Sect. 4). Where a *compilation work* is created, the person who has created it by combining works or parts of works, has copyright thereto. This does not limit the rights to the individual works (Sect. 5).

58. Section 7 contains a presumption rule providing that the person whose name or generally known *pseudonym or signature* is stated in the usual manner on copies of the work is presumed to be the author.

II. Joint Works/Works Created by Several Persons

59. Works are often results of co-operation between several persons. Where the individual contributions cannot be separated a joint proprietorship is created.[1] Section 6 provides that if a work has two or more authors whose contributions do not constitute independent works, then the copyright belongs to the authors jointly. Section 6 is not applied where the contributions can be naturally separated, for example the text and the illustrations in a literary work. On the other hand, computer programs, for example, are often created as a result of joint contributions which cannot be separated.

   1. The co-operation may occur either simultaneously or successively, for example when a scientific article is checked by another.

60. Joint proprietors may *only exploit their copyright together*, which requires them to agree in all respects on how to use the copyright. Nevertheless, each of them is free to bring an action for infringement. Co-authors are free to agree on how they arrange their ownership. However, the legal effects of joint proprietorship on copyright are somewhat unclear and it is not clear whether the general principles on joint proprietorship can be applied to copyright.

61. It should be noted that a person who has been merely an *assistant* in the creation of a work cannot acquire copyright. It is not always easy to draw a distinction between authorship and assistance. However, authorship, or co-authorship, requires that the person has contributed to the work by more than merely taking actions based on instructions. Co-authors must be allowed to make their own *artistic decisions*. The contribution of labour and skill of the assistant is insignificant for authorship.[1]

   1. M. Koktvedgaard & M. Levin p. 95.

62. One category of work which may create problems regarding ownership of copyright is *cinematographic works*. In Finnish practice, these have been regarded as compilation works, the producer of which is the author. Thus, unlike the situation in some other countries, the rights are not automatically transferred to the producer, but authorship is defined according to the general rules of copyright protection. Individual rights to the elements of the compilation work are created for every person who has participated in creating the work through their personal creative effort. These persons might include the scriptwriter, the director, the composer of the music and the camera operator, and also others who have contributed some creative effort.[1] The producers' rights are also protected as neighbouring rights pursuant to Section 46a. This provision is discussed in §9.

1. M. Salokannel pp. 145*ff.*

III. Works Made for Hire

63. An *employee acquires initial ownership* of the copyright to a work. However, works enjoying copyright, especially with regard to the press, radio and television, are often made to a large extent within employment relationships.[1] There are no explicit provisions governing copyright within employment but the same general rules governing privately made works also regulate the ownership and authorship of such works. There is no equivalent to the Anglo-Saxon and Anglo-American 'works made for hire' system whereby copyright is generally transferred to the employer. The Finnish system follows the principles of the Continental-European system in which copyright is derived from the physical authors, the employees. Even though there is a huge difference in principle between the two systems, in practice the difference is not so great.

1. Employment relationship here also refers to the engagements of civil servants.

64. The parties are free to agree on the transfer of economic rights.[1] Even though no such transfer has been explicitly agreed, an *implied agreement* between the parties may be considered to exist.

1. Please *see* §5, I for transfer of moral rights.

65. Unless otherwise agreed, the general rule is that the employer acquires the right *to freely exploit the work within the employer's field of activities*.[1] The rights are not transferred to a wider degree than is necessary for the employer's normal activities. Even though the employee may freely use those rights which do not fall within the employer's field of activities, the employee may not compete or cause prejudice to the employer when using those rights.

1. The employer's rights are normally exclusive.

66. The scope of the employer's field of activities depends on the nature and terms of the job as well as on custom and general conditions in the business concerned. In some fields almost all rights are transferred to the employer, for example

the business of map-making at the National Survey Board, whereas in other fields no rights are transferred, for example in respect of persons engaged in research work at universities.[1] Normally the situation is somewhere in between. For example, it is clear that newspapers are free to publish the articles which their journalists have written in course of their employment.[2] Where the parties have not agreed on the transfer of rights, the scope of the transfer must be determined on a case-by-case basis depending on the circumstances. Since practice varies greatly between different fields, it is difficult to construct any general rules on how to decide the matter.

1. Committee Report 187:7 p. 128.
2. However, the situation is more complicated in the case of freelance journalists.

67. *The employer's right to use the work continues as before, even after the employment is terminated.* In accordance with the general rule provided in Section 28, the employer may neither *alter* the work nor *transfer* the rights to others, unless otherwise agreed. However, the rights may be transferred to another party if they are transferred together with the business in which they are exploited.

68. *Computer programs.* Section 40b provides an important exception to the rule that the employee has initial title to works made in employment relationships. This exception provides that where a computer program and a work directly associated with it have been created within the scope of the duties of an employment relationship, then the copyright to the program and the work shall pass to the employer.[1] It should be noted that this provision follows from the general rule on works created within employment relationships in that the moral rights are transferred and in that the rights are transferred permanently.[2] Section 40b, paragraph 2 provides that this provision is not applicable to programs or to works created by persons engaged in teaching or research at universities or the like.

1. This complies with Art. 2(3) of the EC Directive 91/250 on the Legal Protection of Computer Programs.
2. In this respect Finnish law, contrary to Swedish law, the EC Directive, since the latter applies only to economic rights. It has also been argued that the transfer of moral rights might be contrary to Art. 6*bis* of the Berne Convention (M. Koktvedgaard & M. Levin p. 106).

69. Section 40b is applied correspondingly to the right to databases as provided in Section 49. Section 27, paragraph 3 provides that Section 40b shall be applied only where not otherwise agreed.

70. *Commissioned works.* The general provisions on authorship and transfer of rights also apply to commissioned works, so that authors have copyright to works which they have created. Section 27, paragraph 2 provides that the transfer of a copy does not include a transfer of copyright. Consequently where, for example, a painter has painted a unique oil-painting on commission, he has copyright to the painting and may thus make copies of it. Nevertheless, the parties may agree, explicitly or implicitly, to the contrary. The view taken in the *travaux préparatoires* is that in the case of a unique painting made on commission, the presumption is that the painter has waived his rights to make copies of the painting.

71. Section 27, paragraph 2 provides that in the case of a *portrait* created on commission, the author may not exercise his rights without the permission of the person portrayed and of the person who commissioned the portrait. Furthermore, where a photographic portrait has been created on commission, the person portrayed has the right to authorise the inclusion of the portrait in a newspaper, periodical or bibliographical work, unless otherwise explicitly agreed (Sect. 40c).

§5. Transfer

I. Assignment of Copyright[1]

72. Copyright is basically regarded as another property right. The economic rights of a copyright may be freely transferable. There are no formal requirements on an agreement on the assignment or licensing of copyright. Assignments are also often made by *implied agreements*. There are no requirements for registration and copyright may be freely *mortgaged*.

SC 1992:63 (Kalevala Koru)
The Supreme Court held that a designer of jewellery had not transferred his rights to the organisers of a competition in which the designer had participated with the jewellery, on being presented with a prize in the competition.

1. The rules on assignment of neighbouring rights are the same as those for assignment of copyright, unless otherwise stated.

73. The economic rights may be transferred in whole or in part (Sect. 27, paragraph 1).[1] However, the author cannot transfer to another the *moral rights* defined in Section 3.[2] The author is not bound by an agreement to transfer these moral rights. However, he may waive his moral rights with binding effect with regard to uses which are limited in character and extent. The transferee's rights are further limited by a presumption rule in Section 28. This provides that the transferee may not *alter the work or transfer* the copyright to others without the consent of the author.

1. Licences are considered below in §5, II.
2. Note the discussion on moral rights in computer programs (and databases) in Sect. 40b.

74. Section 27, paragraph 2 provides that the transfer of a copy does not include a transfer of the copyright.[1] Thus, for example, a buyer of a sculpture may not make postcards of the same sculpture. However, the parties may agree that the economic rights are also transferred. Such an agreement may also be made implicitly.

Court of Appeal of Helsinki decision of 23 May 1978 (Sailing boat)
The defendant had given the plaintiff the exclusive right to manufacture and sell a sailing boat which he had designed. The Court held that in so doing the defendant had not transferred to the plaintiff the copyright to the sailing boat.

1. Please *see* the paragraph concerning exceptions with regard to portraits made on commission.

75. An agreement by which the author transfers the rights to *future works* is binding. The rules on initial authorship also apply to such works. However, where a term of an agreement on transfer of rights, especially with regard to agreements concerning future works of an author, becomes unreasonable it may be adjusted by the court as provided in Section 36 of the Contracts Act.[1]

1. Oikeustoimilaki ['Acts in Law Act'] No. 228 of 1929.

76. Succession. As long as the author lives, he alone disposes of the copyright. It does not, therefore, constitute a part of marital property. After his death, the rules governing marital rights to property, inheritance and wills apply to copyright. All the rights of the author, including the moral rights, are transferred to the successors, the surviving spouse and testamentary heirs. The author may issue binding directions in his will as to the exercise of the copyright (Sect. 41).

77. Distraint. Special restrictions apply to distraint of copyright and copyrights forming part of a bankrupt's estate. Section 42 provides that copyright shall not be subject to distraint as long as the copyright remains with the author. The same also applies where the copyright is held by any person who has acquired it through marital right to property, inheritance or bequest. This rule applies only to copyright, i.e. the copies of a work may be taken in execution. However, manuscripts and works of art that have not been exhibited, placed on sale or otherwise authorised for dissemination may not be taken in execution where they are in the possession of the author or of any person who has acquired them by virtue of marital right to property, inheritance or bequest.

78. The prohibition of distraint applies only to the copyright itself and, in case of non-disseminated manuscripts or works of art, to the copies. Therefore, royalties and other rights based on the copyright may be taken in execution in the usual manner. The prohibition protects only the interests of the author and his successors, etc. Thus, where the author has transferred the copyright to another, the copyright is not exempt from distraint. Even though Section 42 refers only to the prohibition of distraint, the same rules apply with regard to *bankruptcy*.[1]

1. H. Olsson pp. 236*ff.*

II. Licences

79. Generally speaking, assignments and licences are governed by the same rules in Finnish copyright law. The parties may freely determine the terms of a licence. The Copyright Act contains some provisions on *public performance contracts* (Sect. 30), *publishing contracts* (Sects. 31 to 38) and *film contracts* (Sects. 39 to 40). Since these provisions are non-mandatory and the parties may freely agree otherwise, they will not be considered in this context. Contractual and compulsory licences are discussed below.

80. It has been held that the terms of a licence are to be interpreted restrictively when determining the scope of the rights included in the licence. The general rule is that any rights which have not, explicitly or implicitly, been transferred to the licensee, remain in the licensor's possession. Thus, the rights that are transferred should be clearly specified. General assignments and licences, i.e. assignments whereby all rights are transferred *en bloc*, are not invalid as such, but the assignment is presumed not to be general unless the parties have clearly agreed otherwise.[1]

   1. M. Koktvedgaard & M. Levin p. 97.

81. A problem may arise where *new forms of exploiting* a copyright have arisen after entering into a general assignment/licence. The prevailing opinion is that in such cases the right to exploit the copyright in respect of the new forms is held by the assignee/licensee if the author was or should have been aware of the new forms of exploitation. Otherwise the said rights are held by the author.[1] With regard to the problems that might arise because the term of protection was extended from 50 years to 70 years, *see* §8 below.

   1. P.-L. Haarmann (1992) p. 218.

82. A general principle of intellectual property law provides that the parties to an agreement have a *duty of loyalty*. Each party has an obligation not to take actions obstructing the other from exercising his rights and the assignor/licensor may not use the rights that remain in his possession in a manner that would diminish the value of the transferred rights.[1]

   1. M. Koktvedgaard & M. Levin p. 98.

83. Contractual licences. It would be very difficult for many authors individually to enforce their copyrights against the users, for example television and radio broadcasters. In view of this, authors have founded *collecting societies*,[1] which represent the authors in matters of copyright.[2] The users, for their part, agree with the collecting societies on the terms of use of the works and on royalties. The copyright societies then collect the royalties from the users and distribute them to the authors. However, since not all authors have transferred their rights to the collecting societies, it would be difficult for users to determine in each case whether the authors have transferred their rights to the collecting societies. Therefore the Copyright Act provides that in some cases the societies shall also represent those authors who have not transferred their rights. Thus, the societies represent all authors regardless of whether or not they have entered into agreements with the authors, and the system therefore falls somewhere between a system with compulsory licences and a system with voluntary licences.

   1. The most important collecting societies in Finland are Teosto ry, Kopiosto ry, Gramex ry and Kuvasto ry. Teosto represents composers, arrangers, lyric writers, translators of lyrics and publishers associated with musical works. Gramex represents performing artists and producers of musical works. Kopiosto deals with the photocopying of works as well as with unabridged and simultaneous retransmission of radio and television transmissions. Kuvasto represents painters and other artists working in the visual arts (R. Hilli p. 128).
   2. The collecting society referred to in Sects. 13, 14, 25f, 25h and 26 is Kopiosto ry.

84. The system of contractual licences applies to photocopying, to reproduction in educational activities and to radio and television transmissions. Section 13 provides that anyone who has received authorisation from a collecting society in a certain field to make copies of published works by *photocopying*, also has the right to make copies of works in the same field, the author of which is not represented by the collecting society. The same terms apply to both kinds of reproduction.

85. Section 14 concerns *reproduction in educational activities*. It provides that whenever a collecting society in a certain field has given authorisation for the making of copies by audio or video recording of a disseminated work included in a radio or television transmission, for use in educational activities or in scientific research, then the party so authorised may also make copies on corresponding terms of a work in the same field, included in a transmission, the author of which is not represented by the society. The provision does not apply to educational activities conducted for commercial purposes (Sect. 54a).

86. Sections 25f and 25h concern *radio and television transmissions*. Both provisions were harmonised with the Satellite Broadcasting Directive in 1995.[1] A radio or television transmitting organisation may, where it has entered into an agreement with a collecting society on the right to transmit works in a certain field, also transmit a work within the same field by an author who is not represented by the society. The provision does not, however, apply to a dramatic work, a cinematographic work, or to any other work where the author has prohibited the transmission. Nor does the provision apply to works which are retransmitted simultaneously with the original transmission without any change in the transmission. Nevertheless, the provision applies to transmissions by satellite only where the satellite transmission is simultaneous with the terrestrial transmission by the same broadcaster (Section 25f).

1. Council Directive 93/83/EEC of 27 September 1993 on the co-ordination of certain rules concerning copyright and rights related to copyright applicable to satellite broadcasting and cable retransmission.

87. Section 25h concerns *simultaneous retransmissions*. A broadcaster may, where it has entered into agreement with a collecting society in a certain field on the right to retransmit works simultaneously with the original work without any changes in the work, also retransmit a work within the same field by an author who is not represented by the society.

88. Section 26 concerns the rights to royalties of those authors who have not entered into an agreement with the collecting society. The same stipulations issued by the collecting society concerning authors' rights to remuneration apply to those authors who are not represented by the collecting society as apply to those authors who are so represented. However, even if the stipulations do not provide, for the authors represented by the society, the right to individual remuneration, an author who is not represented by the society has the right to claim individual remuneration from the society. Where the parties cannot agree on the terms of the contractual licences in cases concerning Sections 13, 14 and 25h, the dispute is to be settled by an arbitration tribunal (Sect. 54).

89. Compulsory licences. In some cases the authors' rights are restricted even more than in the case of contractual licences. Certain provisions in the Copyright Act also permit certain kinds of use of protected works without authorisation from the author or from a collecting society. In such cases, the authors are entitled to remuneration from the users. However, since the users of the works are not obliged to notify the authors or their representatives of the said use, it is difficult for the authors to find out about the use and thus their rights are rather weak.[1] The provisions on compulsory licences are contained in Sections 18, 19 and 25i.

1. P.-L. Haarmann (1992) p. 155.

90. Section 18 concerns *compilation works for use in education.* It provides that minor parts of literary or musical works may be incorporated into a compilation work, intended for use in education after five years have elapsed since the original works were published. In connection with a text, a disseminated work of art may be represented in pictorial form. However, Section 18 is not applicable when the original works were explicitly created for use in education.

91. Section 19, paragraph 4 concerns *lending of copies to the public.* It provides, pursuant to the general rule of the Rental Directive,[1] that the author has the right to remuneration where copies of a work are loaned to the public. This provision, however, is subject to important exceptions.[2] Firstly, it does not apply to products of architecture, artistic handicraft or industrial art. Secondly, it does not apply to lending from public libraries or from libraries serving research or educational services. Remuneration may be claimed only for loans which have taken place during the three preceding calendar years.

1. Council Directive 92/100 of 19 November 1992 on rental right and lending right and on certain rights related to copyright in the field of intellectual property.
2. Article 5 of the Directive allows the Member States to derogate from the exclusive public lending right.

92. Section 25i concerns *simultaneous retransmission of radio and television programmes by cable.* It provides that a cable operator may retransmit by wire, simultaneously with the original transmission and without making any change in the transmission, works transmitted by the Finnish Broadcasting Company (Oy Yleisradio Ab).[1] Remuneration is paid through a collecting society and must be claimed within three years counted from the end of the year in which the transmission occurs.[2]

1. Section 16 of the Cable Transmission Act as amended by Act 1213 of 4 December 1992. Note that cable operators are obliged to retransmit the transmissions referred to in Sect. 16 of the Act.
2. The collecting society referred to is Kopiosto ry.

§6. SCOPE OF EXCLUSIVE RIGHTS

I. Moral Rights

93. The Copyright Act provides for four different kinds of protection for the moral rights of the author (*droit moral*). Firstly, the author has the right to be acknowledged as the author (*droit à la paternité*). Secondly, the author has the right to object to derogatory treatment (*droit au respect*). Thirdly, special protection exists for classic works. Finally, since 1995 authors have had a right of access, allowing them to see works which they have transferred (*droit d'accès*).

94. It has been argued that there exists a *droit de repentir* in contractual relationships. This means that the author has the right in some circumstances to prevent the publication of a work by buying up the copies which have already been made (*droit de retrait*), together with the right to make alterations when publishing a new edition (*droit de modifier*).[1] *The right of disclosure* or *the right to make a work available to the public* is regarded in Finland as an economic right. The mandatory prohibition on alteration or transfer of the work in Section 28, the obligation of the publisher to publish the work in Section 33 and the provision in Section 42 that copyright cannot be subject to legal seizure might also be included under the heading of moral rights in a broad sense.[2]

1. P.-L. Haarmann (1992) p. 111.
2. J. Rosén pp. 358*ff*.

95. *Droit à la paternité*. Section 3, paragraph 1 provides that the name of the author must be stated in the manner required by proper usage when copies of a work are made or when the work is made available to the public. It should be noted that it may be required only that the name be stated in the manner required by proper usage. What is considered to be a manner required by proper usage is determined on practical grounds and varies between different categories of work. In churches, for example, it would not be appropriate to read the name of the composers of the hymns. The same applies to music used in such contexts as restaurants and commercials. The right is also quite restricted concerning works of technical character, i.e. industrial designs, computer programs, etc. Where the work has been made by several authors jointly (joint authorship), all the authors must be mentioned.[1]

1. See e.g. *Court of Appeal of Turku judgment of 2 August 1985* and *Court of Appeal of Helsinki judgment of 30 September 1987*.

96. The name of the author must be stated regardless of the extent to which the work is made available to the public. The author must also be stated in accordance with proper usage where a work is *cited* (Sect. 22). A mere reference to the author is not sufficient. Instead, the source must be mentioned and the work must be identified, for example by stating the title, publisher and date of publication.

97. *Droit au respect*. Section 3, para. 2 provides that a work may not be *altered* in a manner which is prejudicial to the author's literary or artistic reputation, or to his individuality. Furthermore, the work may not be made *available to the public* in

such a form or context. What is regarded as prejudicial to the author's literary and artistic reputation is assessed in the first hand on objective grounds, but the subjective view of the author is also given some attention. Even though the provision refers only to a work,[1] it is also applied to a copy of a work.[2]

SC 1974 II 49 (Dirty hands)
The Finnish translation of a French dramatic work had been altered to reflect the views of the artistic director and the director. The Supreme Court held that the alterations were prejudicial to the translator's literary and artistic reputation and to his individuality. The art director, the director and the theatre were ordered to pay damages to the translator.

1. For example the translation of a literary work is of inferior quality.
2. For example a painting or sculpture is altered in a manner which is prejudicial to the author's reputation.

98. A work may be altered or made available to the public in such a way that it offends the ideological values of the author, for example a musical work representing a certain ideological position may be made available with words reflecting an opposing ideology. However, parodies, travesties, etc. have traditionally been allowed and the authors can do nothing but accept them.

99. Chapter 2 of the Copyright Act contains some rules governing alterations of works. Section 25e provides an exemption to the general rule in Section 3, paragraph 2. It provides that buildings and items for use may be altered by the owner without the consent of the author where considerations of a technical nature or reasons connected with their use so require. The provisions on computer programs provide that such alterations may be made which are necessary for the use of computer programs in the intended manner (Sect. 25j). There is a non-mandatory rule which provides that the transferee in contractual relationships may not alter a work that has been transferred (Sect. 28).[1]

1. This rule applies only to a work itself, and not to the copies of a work.

100. Classic works. After the death of the author, the moral rights are transferred to the author's successors. However, these might have no interest in protecting the moral rights of the author. In view of this, Section 53 provides that where a work is the subject of public action in a manner which offends against cultural interests, such action may be prohibited. It should be noted that the provision is applied irrespective of the fact that the copyright is no longer in force, or that copyright may not even have existed.

101. This provision refers to cultural interests, not to moral rights as provided in Section 3. Therefore, the requirements for application of the provision have been set at a rather high level.[1]

1. The Ministry of Education, and later the Supreme Court, held that the language of the translations of Alice in Wonderland, Robinson Crusoe and another work were of such poor quality and the story had been changed and abridged to such an extent that cultural interests had been infringed (*SC 1967 II 10*).

102. Droit d'accès. In 1995 the Copyright Act was amended by a new Section 52a on *droit d'accès*.[1] This provides that authors of works of fine art have a right of access allowing them to see any works which they have assigned, provided that this is necessary for the authors' artistic activity or for the purpose of overseeing their economic rights. The successors of an author have the same rights as the author with regard to overseeing economic rights. Nevertheless, the provision is not applicable where the right of access would cause unreasonable inconvenience to the owner or holder of the work. The right is not restricted in time.

 1. It might be noted that even before the amendment it was held that the author might have *droit d'accès. See SC 1976 II 51.*

103. An author must have a proper reason in order to secure the right of access to a work. Such a reason might be, for example, a need to study the technical or artistic solutions used in the work. In order to exercise their economic rights, authors may, for example, take pictures of their work. They may also require that the work be moved for analysis, photography, etc., provided that so doing will not damage the work. The author has no right of access where there are other ways to study the work or to exercise the economic rights.

II. Exploitation Rights

104. Section 2 concerns the economic rights of copyright. It provides that copyright includes the exclusive right to control the work by making copies thereof and by making it available to the public. The exclusive right extends to only those two forms of utilisation, i.e. to making copies and to making the work available to the public. Copyright thus provides no general right to utilise the work. However, in practice those two forms comprise all of the relevant economic rights. In Finnish copyright law the right to make a work available to the public is further divided into public performing rights, the right to distribute copies to the public – which is discussed in connection with reproduction rights, and the right of public exhibition of a work – which is discussed in connection with performing rights.

105. It should be noted that the exclusive rights are restricted by the provisions of Chapter 2 of the Copyright Act. These are discussed in detail below in §2.

A. Reproduction Rights

106. The copyright holder has the exclusive right to make copies of a work. Copying a work means reproducing it in material form. This concerns all categories and types of works which are capable of reproduction. It also concerns all kinds of reproduction, for example photocopying a book or writing a poem on paper. Section 2, paragraph 2 provides that recording a work on a device whereby it can be copied is considered to be reproduction. Thus, saving a work in the memory of a computer or copying it onto a disc, recording a motion picture on videotape, etc. are also considered to be copying. A musical work may be reproduced by recording it, by writing down the notes on paper, by copying the recording, etc. Copies of works of art include copies made by painting and photography, copies in books and postcards, etc. All works which have been made by reproducing another work are considered to be copies, regardless of the form in which the copy is made or how it is reproduced.

107. The definition of a copy does not depend on the extent to which a work has been reproduced. Thus, if a short extract of a poem is included in another work, a small segment of a painting is included in another or a refrain from a song is included in another song, then this is also considered to be reproduction. Even quotations are, in a strict sense, regarded as copies.[1]

Court of Appeal of Helsinki judgment of 9 January 1985 (Exercise book)
The plaintiffs had made an exercise book including exercises and some hints and advice. The defendant had later distributed handouts on a training-course, with himself indicated as the author. These handouts included four exercises which had been included in the said exercise book. The Court held that the defendant had infringed the plaintiffs' copyright and ordered him to pay damages.
SC 1980 II 46 (Housing exhibition)
The defendant had made a photographic enlargement of an article in a newspaper and exhibited the enlargement at a housing exhibition. The Court held that exhibiting the enlargement was not prohibited as public exhibition of a work. However, by making the enlargement of the article, the defendant had infringed the copyright by reproducing the article. The defendant was ordered to pay damages for unauthorised use and other losses.

1. However, note that Sect. 22 provides that quotation is allowed in accordance with proper usage.

108. Generally speaking, there is no difference of status between the original and reproductions of a work. The original manuscript of a book is protected in the same way as the copies of the book. However, Section 52 provides that the copies of a work of art must be marked in such a manner that they cannot be confused with the original work and, furthermore, the name or signature of the author must not be placed onto a copy of a work in such a manner that the copy could be confused with the original work.

109. The right to distribute copies to the public reinforces the author's exclusive right to reproduction in cases where a work has been copied without authorisation. In such cases the author may prevent the distribution of copies. Distribution is defined extensively and includes sale, loan, rental, donation, exchange, etc. Where a copy of a work has been sold or otherwise permanently transferred with the consent of the author, it may be further distributed (Sect. 19, para. 1). However, the work may not be rented, except for products of architecture, artistic handicraft and industrial art, and cinematographic works and computer programs may neither be rented nor loaned.

110. The right to distribute is also important for the author since the author may thereby decide at what time a work is made available to the public.[1] It is also important for the exhaustion of rights.[2] Normally where an author has assigned the right to make copies it is assumed that the assignment also includes the right to distribute the copies.

1. In some other countries this is considered to be a moral right (H. Olsson p. 62).
2. Exhaustion of copyright is discussed in detail below in §7.

B. Performing Rights

111. The *right to public performance* is important mainly for musical, dramatic and cinematographic works. Public performance means that the work is performed or presented either directly in a live event or through an intermediary, for example a motion picture is played on television or recorded music is played in a restaurant. The provision applies only to *public* performance and thus private performance is not restricted.

112. The distinction between public and private is not always clear. The general rule is that a performance is public where the audience is not specified in advance, regardless of whether an entrance fee or other payment is demanded. A performance to which anybody has access is always public. A performance is public, for example, where anybody who is a member of a club or association has access and the club or association has a considerable number of members. Also, if anybody may acquire membership, then the performance is considered to be public even though the audience would in fact be small. Performances of private character, such as family and other strictly private parties, or performances for closed groups, are usually not public. There is considerable body of case law on what is held to be public and what is not.

Court of Appeal of Vaasa decision of 15 April 1986
(A) had several times presented purchased and rented video films in his own apartment for invited guests. (A) had charged the guests 5 marks in order to cover his expenses.[1] The Court held that the performances had taken place in circumstances similar to private parties held at home and that the authors' consent for the performances were thus not required.

1. 5 Finnish marks is about 1 US Dollar.

113. Section 2, paragraph 3 provides that a performance which takes place within the framework of commercial activities for a comparatively large closed group is also considered to be public. This refers mainly to so called industrial music, where music is played in shops, on shop floors, in buses, etc. Even music played on the radio in a taxi has been considered to be a public performance.

114. The author has the *right to exhibit the work publicly*. This is important mainly for works of visual art.[1] It means that a painting, for example, may be put in an exhibition, displayed in a public place, shown on television, etc. only with the consent of the author.

> 1. It should be noted that a motion picture is not exhibited but performed.

C. Adaptation Rights

115. Copyright protects the individual and creative expressive form of ideas, subjects, etc. It is the particular expression making up a work which is protected. Therefore, copyright does not protect the idea or subject itself. Neither does it protect principles, theories, facts or result of research, etc. However, the protection does extend not only to the form in which the work was originally presented (original form) but also to altered forms, i.e. to translations and adaptations, to other literary or artistic forms, and to any other forms created by other technical means, provided that the adapted and the original work can be considered to be the same.

116. Thus, even though a translator, for example, has the exclusive right to the translation itself, these rights do not restrict the rights of the author (Sect. 4, para. 1).[1] The author still has the exclusive right to the work and the rights of the translator are dependent upon the rights of the author, which means that the translator cannot exercise his rights without the consent of the author. Only where a work has been created in free connection with the original work and can be regarded as new and independent, is the copyright to the new work not subject to the copyright to the original work (Sect. 4, para. 2).

> 1. The translation, adaptation, etc., must meet the requirements for a work.

117. For example, the turning of a story into a ballet, the turning of a literary work into a dramatic work and the making of a fabric from a knitting pattern are regarded as adaptations. On the other hand where, for example, a novel is turned into a painting, a poem is turned into music or a photograph is used as the model for a painting the matter does not concern an adaptation, but rather a new and independent work.[1]

Copyright Council 1986:12
The making of diapositives of photographs in a book was held to be reproduction of the photographs and therefore required the authorisation of the photographer. Where the photographs presented works that were protected by copyright, authorisation was required both from the copyright holder of the protected works and from the photographer.

> 1. P.-L. Haarmann (1992) p. 74.

118. When assessing whether a work is new and independent, the similarities between works are evaluated. The decisive factor is that of how similar the works are considered to be and whether the works provide the same experience and feeling. However, even though the similarities between the works might be striking, the later work is not necessarily an adaptation of the earlier work where the authors have used the same sources for their works.

Copyright Council 1995:12 (Sculpture)
Two sculptors had used a famous Finnish skier in a certain competition as the subject of their works. Even though there were many similarities between the two sculptures, it was not held that the later one was an adaptation of the earlier one, since the subject of a work is not protected and it was probable that two sculptures with the same subject would resemble one another.

D. Translation Rights

119. Generally speaking, the same rules apply to translations as to other kinds of adaptations. It is clear from Sections 2 and 4 that translations and adaptations are treated in the same way. This means that the translator's rights depend upon those of the author.[1]

1. See §6, II, C above concerning adaptation rights.

E. Other Rights

1. Droit de Suite

120. The 1995 amendment included provisions on *resale remuneration* or *droit de suite* in the Copyright Act by appending the new Sections 26i to 26m. Section 26i provides that the author has the right to receive, in resale remuneration, five per cent of the sales price for the professional and public resale of works of fine art.[1] The expression 'professional and public resale' refers to sale by auction, by art galleries and by art dealers. Thus, the provision is not applied to trade between private persons. The provision refers to resale, which means that it is not applied to the initial sale, for example when a work to which the author still has title is sold on commission by a gallery on behalf of the author.

1. The price is calculated exclusive of VAT.

121. Resale remuneration is paid only for the sale of works of fine art, which refers to pictorial art, sculptures, works of textile art, graphic art, installations, video art, etc., as well as to artistic handicrafts and industrial arts, provided that these have been produced in only a single copy (a unique work). However, there is no right to remuneration for the sale of products of architecture and photographic works.

122. This right remains in force for the same term as a copyright and is not transferable. After the author's death, however, the rights are transferred to his successors pursuant to Section 41. Such rights may not be subject to legal seizure, but any actual remuneration paid may be seized.

123. The remuneration is collected and distributed by a collecting society. The right lapses if the claim for remuneration has not been submitted to the collecting society within three years counted from the end of the year in which the work was sold. The payment of remuneration is the obligation of the seller or of the intermediary (Sect. 26k).

124. The provisions on resale remuneration are applied where the author is a national of a state belonging to the EEA,[1] or is habitually resident in such a state (Sect. 63). Authors from other states may acquire resale remuneration in Finland on the basis of reciprocity.[2]

1. The European Economic Area.
2. Government Bill No. 287 of 1994 pp. 58*ff.*, pp. 77*ff.*

2. Public Lending Right

125. Section 19, paragraph 1 provides that when a copy of a work has been sold or otherwise transferred with the consent of the author, then it may be distributed further. Thus copies of works, except for cinematographic works and computer programs, may be loaned. Section 19, paragraph 4 provides that the author has the right to remuneration for the loan of copies of a work to the public. This provision, however, does not apply to lending from public libraries or from libraries serving research or educational services.[1] Thus the authors receive no remuneration for public lending.[2]

1. The exemption complies with Art. 5 of the Rental Directive.
2. Instead of remuneration for public lending, there is a system of awards and financial support for authors of books and for translators. This system clearly lies outside of the copyright system.

3. Others

126. Blank tape levy. There is a special levy on blank video- and audiotapes in order to compensate authors for reduced sales of their works due to private recording. Where a blank video- or audiotape, or any other similar device suitable for private use and recording, is produced or imported for the purpose of distribution to the public, the manufacturer or importer must pay a levy. The levy, which is paid on the basis of the playing time of the tapes, is paid to authors as compensation.[1] Such compensation is paid in the form of individual compensation and is also used for purposes benefiting authors jointly. The levy is collected and distributed by a collecting society.[2]

1. In 1996 the levy was 3 pennies per minute for audiotape and 4.5 pennies per minute for videotape (100 pennies = 1 mark = about 0.2 USD).
2. The collecting society referred to is Teosto (Finnish composers' copyright society).

§7. Limitation to or Exemptions from the Scope of Copyright Protection

127. The limitations and exemptions in the scope of protection conferred by Section 2 are included in Chapter 2 of the Act (Sects. 11 to 26). Exclusive rights are limited in three different ways. Firstly, an exemption may give another party a free right to use certain rights in certain circumstances. Secondly, in some circumstances a work may be used without the consent of the author, but the author has a right to remuneration. This system is referred to in the Nordic literature as compulsory licencing. Thirdly, the authors' rights may be limited by the system of contractual licences. In such a system the user makes an agreement on the use of works with a collecting society representing all authors, regardless of whether or not they have entered into any agreement with the collecting society. Contractual licences and compulsory licences are discussed above in §5, II.

128. The limitations and exemptions of Chapter 2 apply only to disseminated or published works. Therefore, where a work has not been disseminated or published it is normally protected against all forms of use.[1] Section 8 provides that a work is considered to be disseminated when it has been lawfully made available to the public and that it is considered to be published when copies thereof have, with the consent of the author, been placed on sale or otherwise distributed to the public.[2]

1. M. Koktvedgaard & M. Levin p. 150.
2. The expression 'made available to the public' has the same content as the same expression in Sect. 2.

129. A general rule of interpretation prescribes that provisions on limitations and exemptions to copyright are to be interpreted narrowly. They must also be interpreted in accordance with the provisions of the Berne Convention.[1]

1. P.-L. Haarmann (1992) pp. 117–119.

130. Section 11 provides that the exemptions provided in Chapter 2 of the Copyright Act, with the exception of alterations to buildings and useful articles, do not restrict moral rights.

131. Exhaustion. The provisions of Sections 19 and 20 concerning exhaustion of copyright are, perhaps, the most important limitations on copyright protection. If, with the consent of the author, a copy of a work has been sold or otherwise permanently transferred, or if the work has likewise been published, then the copy may be further distributed and the work may be publicly exhibited. It should be noted that the rights are exhausted only where the copy has been transferred or published with the consent of the author and, therefore, these rules cannot be applied for example to copies made for private use or to pirated goods. Furthermore, it is required that the copies have been permanently transferred. Thus the rights are not exhausted where the copies have been loaned or rented (without being sold beforehand).

132. Exhaustion applies to copies of a work, not to the work itself. Where the rights have been exhausted the author may no longer dispose of the rights to the copy. Copies may be re-sold, loaned, etc., but they may not, for example, be reproduced or performed publicly.[1] Section 20 provides that such copies may also be publicly exhibited. However, lending rights are not exhausted for copies of cinematographic works and computer-readable computer programs. Furthermore, copies of works may not be made available to the public by rental or by any comparable act in law, for example a sale with a right of repurchase. Nevertheless, a product of architecture, artistic handicrafts, or industrial arts may be rented to the public.[2]

1. Lending is, however, subject to compulsory licencing. Please see §5, II above.
2. Section 19 was amended in 1995 in order to meet the requirements of the Rental Directive.

133. The rules on exhaustion are mandatory. Even though the author may agree with the transferee about the exhaustion of rights with regard to a permanent transfer of a copy, and that the said agreement is binding between the parties, such an agreement is usually not binding on any third party who has acquired a copy from the original transferee.[1]

1. M. Koktvedgaard & M. Levin pp. 119–120.

134. It has been the traditional view in Finland that copyrights are *exhausted globally*, i.e. that the rights are exhausted regardless of the country in which the copies were originally permanently transferred. However, the recent development of EC law has, at least partially, changed this situation. Thus, pursuant to Article 9 (2) of the Rental Directive, *neighbouring rights*, as provided in Sections 45, 46, 46a and 48, are subject to *Community exhaustion*, i.e. they are exhausted only where the work has been transferred within the European Economic Area (EEA).[1] Also, Article 4 (c) of the Computer Program Directive[2] provides that computer programs are subject to Community exhaustion. In the Finnish *travaux préparatoires*, however, it was regarded that this does not mean that global exhaustion is excluded and therefore it was held that computer programs are still subject to global exhaustion in Finnish law.[3]

1. Government Bill 1994/287 p. 72.
2. Council Directive 91/250/EEC of 14 May 1991 on the legal protection of computer programs.
3. Government Bill 1994/287 pp. 41*ff*. However, the Swedish Copyright Act explicitly provides that computer programs are subject to community exhaustion.

135. As a result, neighbouring rights nowadays enjoy stronger protection than the copyright itself, which leads to some odd consequences, for example in the case of musical records. The situation must be regarded as not fully satisfactory, and furthermore, may be inconsistent with EC law.[1] Therefore, it has been argued that copyright should also be subject to Community exhaustion in Finland.

1. The Computer Program Directive.

136. Reproduction for private use. The general and classical principle that the private use of a work is not subject to copyright constitutes an important exemption to copyright protection. Section 12 provides general permission to make copies for private use. It provides that anyone may make *a few copies* of a disseminated work for his own *private use*. However, the provision is not applicable to *computer programs or to works of architecture*. Computer programs are discussed in greater detail below.

137. It should be noted that Section 12 applies only to disseminated works. Thus, where a work has not been disseminated it may not be reproduced even for private use. Also, the provision applies to reproduction only. However, Section 2 provides (indirectly) that a work may be performed in private.

138. The expression 'private use' refers to the strictly private use of a person, which include copying for purposes including studies, research, hobbies, recreation and other non-commercial activities. Thus all forms of commercial exploitation are excluded. The exemption applies only to private persons and thus copies may not be made for use in companies etc. For example, photocopying for educational purposes at schools, universities, etc. is not considered to be private use. However, copies may be made for the family, friends, etc.

139. The meaning of the expression 'a few copies' varies depending on the circumstances. Normally one to four copies may be regarded as a few copies, but more copies might also be acceptable. Where more copies are made than are needed for private use, this is more than 'a few copies'. The copies may be made using any means. It is also permitted to engage an outsider to make the copies. However, musical and cinematographic works, useful articles, sculptures or copies of any other works of art made by artistic reproduction may not be reproduced by engaging an outsider.[1] The *blank tape levy*, discussed in the end of §6, is intended to compensate authors for lost royalties due to private copying.

   1. However, note that the use of the name or signature of the author of a work of fine art is restricted by Sect. 52.

140. Computer programs and databases. Copying, including private copying, of computer programs or computer readable databases without the consent of the author is prohibited by Section 12, paragraph 4.[1] However, Sections 25j and 25k contain some limitations to the protection of computer programs and databases pursuant to the Computer Program Directive.[2] The rules in Sections 25j and 25k are *mandatory*, i.e. any contractual provision limiting the use of a program pursuant to Sections 25j and 25k is null and void.

   1. The provisions on databases took effect on 15 April 1998.
   2. Council Directive 91/250/EEC of 14 May 1991 on the legal protection of computer programs. The Finnish Copyright Act was harmonised with this directive in 1995.

141. Section 25j provides that anyone who has legally acquired a computer program or database is entitled to prepare such copies of the program or database and make such alterations to the program or database as are necessary for the use thereof for its intended purpose. Furthermore, anyone who has the right to use a program is entitled to prepare necessary back-up copies of it. Finally, anyone who has the right to use a computer program is entitled to observe, study or test the operation of the program in order to determine the ideas and principles which underlie any element thereof (*reverse engineering*). However, it should be noted that no copies may be made for the purpose of reverse engineering.

142. It should also be noted that such copies may be made and used only for the stated purposes. Their use for other purposes is prohibited. Moreover, they may be used only as long as the original copy may be used, i.e. where, for example, the original copy is re-sold or the licencing agreement has terminated, the back-up copy, etc. may no longer be used.[1]

> 1. It may be noted, however, that there is no obligation to destroy such copies.

143. Section 25k concerns the *decompilation of a program*. It provides that the reproduction of the code of a program and the translation of its form is allowed, provided that this is necessary for achieving interoperability with other programs. Thus, the right to decompile covers only the *interfaces* of the program. Decompilation may be performed only by a person authorised to use the program and only when the interface information has not previously been readily available. Furthermore, the information obtained through decompilation may not be used for any purpose other than to achieve interoperability and it may not be transferred to another, except when this is necessary for interoperability. Neither may the said information be used for the development, production or marketing of a program which is substantially similar in expression.

144. Quotation. Section 22 provides that a disseminated work may be quoted, in accordance with proper usage, to the extent which is necessary for the purpose. The provision applies to all kinds of works.[1] It also applies to the rights of performing artists (Sect. 45), the rights of producers (Sects. 46 and 46a), radio and television transmissions (Sect. 48), databases (Sect. 49) and photographs (Sect. 49a).

> 1. P.-L. Haarmann (1992) p. 134. In this respect Swedish law differs from Finnish law. In the Swedish *travaux préparatoires* it was held that the right to quote does not apply to pictorial art. However, compare with Sect. 25.

145. A work may be quoted only insofar as the quotation is 'in accordance with proper usage'. This means that quotations may be used only as an aid to the new work and that there must be an objective connection between the quotations and the new work. Quotations must not be used merely to gild or improve a work. However, it is acceptable for quotations to be used in order to elucidate and illustrate a new text or, for example, to develop the ideas expressed in the quotations. Also, when criticising a work by another person, the said work may be quoted to a greater extent and where quotations are used in, for example, speeches delivered in honour of the occasion. Critics, on the other hand, may be quoted when marketing books, motion pictures, etc. Otherwise it is normally prohibited to include quotations in commercials and advertisements. The consent of the various authors is required for works consisting of quotations only.[1]

> 1. P.-L. Haarmann (1992) p. 135.

146. A work may be quoted to the extent necessary for the purpose. What is considered as necessary extent varies depending on the circumstances. In a scientific or critical work it may be permissible to include relatively extensive quotations, while short works, such as poems, may be quoted in full. In newspapers, for example, quotations may normally be no longer than a couple of lines. In assessing what is considered to be necessary extent, the length of the work including the quotation is irrelevant. It should be noted that the quotation must not be so short that it gives an incorrect impression of its meaning or otherwise becomes misleading. Finally, Section 11, paragraph 2 provides that when a work is used publicly the source must be stated to the extent and in the manner required by proper usage. This also applies to quotations.

147. Current topics and events. Section 23 provides that articles in newspapers and periodicals on current religious, political, or economic topics may be included in other newspapers and periodicals. This provision gives the organs of the press a relatively broad right to quote one another. It applies only to articles on current religious, political or economic events, which means that it is not applicable, for example, to articles on culture or sports, or where the event cannot be considered to be current. However, where reproduction is expressly prohibited there is no such right.

148. Section 25b provides that where a current event is presented in a radio or television transmission or as a film, a work which is visible or audible as part of the current event may be included in the presentation to the extent required for the informational purpose. This provision might be applicable, for example, to the display of paintings in a news program relating to the opening of an exhibition, etc.

149. Public statements and documents. Section 25c provides that oral or written statements submitted in a public representation, before a public authority or at a public meeting concerning matters of public interest may be used without the author's consent.[1] However, such works may be used only in connection with an account of the case or matter in which they were used and, furthermore, only to the extent required for the purpose of such an account. The provision does not apply, for example, to expert opinions. Authors have the exclusive right to publish compilations of their own statements.

1. Compare with Sect. 9 which provides that there is no copyright in laws and decrees, or in decrees and declarations of public authorities and other public bodies. *See above* §2, II.

150. Section 25d provides that copyright does not limit the right, prescribed in law, to acquire information from a public document. This means that both public authorities and individual or corporate persons have the right to make copies of public documents, regardless of whether they are protected by copyright and of whether they have been disseminated. Works may be used, when necessary, in legal proceedings or when national security so requires. Such works and public documents may also be quoted where they have not been disseminated.

151. Use of works of art and buildings. Section 25 provides that disseminated works of art may be reproduced in pictorial form in connection with a text in a critical or scientific presentation, or in a newspaper or a periodical, when reporting on a current event. Thus, the quotation of works of art in pictorial form appears to be more restricted than the quotation of other kinds of works.[1] However, where a copy of a work of art has been permanently transferred or the work has been published, it may be incorporated into a photograph, a motion picture or a television program, provided that such use is of secondary importance.

   1. Government Bill 1994/287 pp. 27*ff.*

152. Section 25a provides that a work of art which is included in a collection exhibited or placed on sale may be reproduced in pictorial form in catalogues and notices pertaining to the exhibition or sale. A work of art may also be photographed where it is permanently situated at, or in the immediate vicinity of, a public place. However, where the work is the principal subject of the picture, the picture must not be used for commercial purposes.[1] Buildings may be freely photographed.

   1. Nevertheless, such a picture may be included in a newspaper or in a periodical where it is connected with a text.

153. Section 25e provides that *buildings and useful articles may be altered* without the consent of the author where this is required due to considerations of a technical nature or for reasons connected with their use.

154. Public performance. Section 21 provides that published works, excluding dramatic and cinematographic works, may be performed in connection with divine services and education. Such works may also be publicly performed on occasions where the performance of the said works is not the main feature of the event, provided that no admission fee is charged and that the event is not arranged for commercial purposes. This provision may also be applied in connection with popular educational activities and for charitable or other non-profit purposes, provided that the performers receive no remuneration for their performance.

155. Concert programs. Where a musical work is performed with a libretto, the libretto may be incorporated into concert programmes etc. provided for the use of the audience. This provision does not apply to texts printed, for example, in newspapers.[1]

   1. P.-L. Haarmann (1992) p. 152.

156. Reproduction in educational activities. Section 14, paragraph 2 provides that teachers or students are permitted to copy a work for temporary use in educational activities and for educational purposes only. A disseminated literary work or a work of art may be incorporated into the matriculation examination or any comparable test.

157. For further details of compulsory licences for the making of copies by audio or video recording of a work included in a radio or television transmission for use in educational activities or in scientific research *see* §5, II above.

158. Reproduction in certain institutions, archives, libraries and museums. Section 15 provides that copies of works included in radio and television transmissions may be made by audio or video recording for the purpose of temporary use in hospitals, old people's homes, prisons and similar institutions.

159. Certain archives, libraries and museums have the right to make copies of a work for the purposes of their activities. Sections 1–6 of the Copyright Decree stipulate further conditions governing such reproduction.

160. Reproduction for handicapped persons. Section 17 provides that copies of published literary or musical works may be made with the purpose of rendering the text readable by visually handicapped persons. Certain institutions have the right to make copies of literary works by means of sound recording for the purpose of lending to handicapped persons or to other persons who, due to illness, cannot use books in the conventional manner.

161. Special provisions on radio and television transmissions. Section 25g, paragraph 1 provides that a transmitting organisation has the right to record a work on a device by which it can be reproduced for use in the organisation's own transmissions, provided that the organisation has the right to transmit the work. This enables the transmitting organisation to make the copy of the work which is necessary for the transmission.

162. A transmitting organisation has a statutory obligation to make a copy of transmitted programs.[1] Thus, Section 25, paragraph 2 provides that a transmitting organisation may, when fulfilling its statutory recording obligation, make a copy of a work included in a transmitted program.

1. Section 6 of the Radio Liability Decree (No. 621 of 1971) and Sect. 21 of the Cable Transmissions Act (No. 307 of 1987).

163. Section 25g, paragraph 3 concerns a kind of *internal use for public authorities, enterprises*, etc. It provides that a public authority, entrepreneur or some other organisation may, for the purposes of internal communication, make a few copies of a work included in a current event or news program which has been transmitted by radio or television. The expression 'a few copies' has the same content as it has in Section 12 governing reproduction for private use.[1]

1. Government Bill 1994/287 p. 76.

§8. Duration of Protection

164. Until 1995 the term of copyright protection in Finland was 50 years. However, in January 1996 the Copyright Act was amended in order to meet the requirements of the Council Directive harmonising the term of copyright.[1]

1. Council Directive (93/98/EC) of 29 October 1993 harmonising the term of protection of copyright and certain related rights.

165. In accordance with the Directive, Section 43 provides that the *term of protection is 70 years* counted from the year following the year in which the author died.[1] In the case of joint proprietorship, as provided in Section 6, the term is counted from the year following the year in which the last surviving author died. For cinematographic works the term is counted from the year following the year in which the last of the following surviving persons died: the principal director, the author of the screenplay, the author of the dialogue and the composer of any music specifically composed for use in the soundtrack.

1. Amended by Act No. 1654 of 22 December 1995. Government Bill 1995/8.

166. Where a work has been disseminated without mentioning the author's name or generally known pseudonym or signature, the term of protection is counted from the year following the year in which the work was disseminated. If the work was published in parts, then the term of protection is counted for each part separately. Where the identity of the author is disclosed during the said period, the term of protection is counted from the year following the year in which the author died. In the case of a non-disseminated work of unknown authorship, the term of copyright is counted from the year following the year in which the work was created (Sect. 44).

167. Pursuant to Article 4 of the Directive, Section 44a provides protection for *previously unpublished works*. Any person who, for the first time, publishes or disseminates a previously unpublished or non-disseminated work, the protection of which has expired in Finland, is entitled to hold economic rights to the work as provided in Section 2. The term of such protection is 25 years.

168. Transition provisions. The new longer term of protection is also applicable to works created before the amendments entered into force. Therefore, even if the protection under the old provisions has expired, the work may acquire extended protection under the new provisions. In practice this means that protection for the works of authors who died between 1926 and 1945 has been re-established.[1] However, it should be noted that expired protection has been re-established only for works which were created within the European Economic Area (EEA) and for certain recordings, as provided in Article 14 of the TRIPS Agreement. Protection for works created outside of the EEA has been extended only where the protection was still effective on 1 January 1996.

1. Article 10 (2) of the Directive was originally not intended to be interpreted in this manner. However, the *Phil Collins* judgment of the European Court of Justice (*Collins v. IMTRAT Handels-GmbH* (C-92/93) [1993] 3 C.M.L.R. 773) changed the situation.

169. Some problems may arise in cases where copyright has been assigned or licenced and the term of protection has thereafter expired and been re-established or extended. There are no explicit provisions stipulating the party to whom the new rights belong, and the situation must be resolved by applying the general rules and principles of copyright and contract law. In the first case, where the copyright has expired, the assignment or licence agreement is presumed to have terminated because the subject of the said agreement, i.e. the copyright, has expired. This would mean that the re-established rights belonged to the author.[1]

1. Government Bill 1995/8 pp. 13ff.

170. Cases in which copyright has been assigned or licenced and the term of protection has subsequently been extended are more complicated. The *travaux préparatoires* from 1953 provide that where the rights have been extended after entering into an agreement, the extended rights belong to the author, except where otherwise explicitly agreed. This, and the intent of the parties, are still the main principles. Moreover, the transition provisions provide that the old term is to be applied to agreements concluded before the amendment. Thus, the extended rights normally belong to the author. However, in some circumstances it may be held that the intent of the parties was also to transfer the extended rights. In such cases the extended rights may belong to the assignee or licensee.[1]

1. Government Bill 1995/8 pp. 11–13.

171. The transition provisions provide that copies which have been made before the amendments entered into force may be distributed or exhibited irrespective of the extended protection. However, the provisions on rental and lending rights, and the *droit de suite*-right are also applicable to such copies.

172. A *transition period* is applicable in some circumstances. Where essential measures were taken in order to use a work the protection of which has now expired, such use may be continued so as to end before the year 2003, despite the re-establishment of protection. However, the provisions on rental and lending rights, and the *droit de suite*-right are also applicable to such use.

173. If, before the amendments took effect, a transmitting organisation has recorded a work, the protection of which has expired, in order to transmit the said work, then the organisation may transmit the work before the year 2003 despite the re-establishment of protection.

§9. NEIGHBOURING RIGHTS

174. Neighbouring rights are regulated in Chapter 5 of the Copyright Act. The provisions on neighbouring rights include several references to the provisions on copyright. Where not otherwise stated, the same general rules apply to neighbouring rights as to copyright. For example, the provisions concerning inheritance, bankruptcy and distraint are the same for both copyright and neighbouring rights.

175. Rights of performing artists. The rights of performing artists are the subject of Sections 45, 47 and 47a. Section 45, paragraph 1 provides that a live performance of a literary or artistic work may not be fixated or made available to the public without the consent of the performing artist.[1] Paragraph 2 provides that a recorded performance may not be copied or distributed to the public without the consent of the artist. The *term of protection* is 50 years counted from the end of the year in which the performance took place or, where the recording has been published or disseminated within this period, 50 years from the end of the year during which the recorded performance was published or disseminated for the first time.

1. The provision defines fixation as something being 'recorded on a device by means of which the performance can be reproduced'.

176. Only artists performing literary or artistic works enjoy protection, but there are no requirements of originality and creativity with regard to such performance. The performances of artists performing other kinds of works are generally not protected, for example clowns, acrobats, conjurers, and so on.[1] However, even though directors are normally regarded as authors and thereby hold copyright, in the case of operas, for example, they have been held to enjoy performers' rights.[2]

1. P.-L. Haarmann (1994) p. 62.
2. *See SC 1987:116.* Note that the Court did not rule on whether the director also enjoyed copyright protection.

177. Performing artists are protected in respect of recording and of radio and television transmissions or other direct communication of their performances. Thus, they do not enjoy protection against alterations, imitations, mimicry, adaptations, etc. Nevertheless, moral rights are also applicable to performers' rights. Moral rights may prohibit the alteration of a performance.[1] The transfer of the right to film a performance comprises, unless otherwise agreed, the right to distribute the recorded performance to the public by lending. Performers' rights are limited by many of the restrictions discussed above in part 7 of this chapter and they are exhausted in the same way as copyright with the exception that they are subject to Community exhaustion.[2] Performing artists are entitled to a share of the tape levy.

1. *See* e.g. *SC 1975 II 37 (Halkola).*
2. Please *see* §7 on exhaustion.

178. Section 47 concerns the right to *remuneration*, and applies to both performing artists and producers. It provides that where a phonograph record or another device on which sound has been recorded is used, directly or indirectly, in radio or television transmission or in any other public performance, a remuneration must be paid to the producer and to the performing artist whose performance has been recorded on the device. Following an amendment in 1995, the provision also applies, for example, to music played in cafés, restaurants, hotels, shops, buses, etc.[1] Where many artists have participated in the performance, they may realise their claim only jointly, and the performer and producer may realise their rights only by submitting their claims together. Where the performers and producers are represented by a collecting society, the claim for remuneration must be submitted within three years counted from the end of the year during which the use took place. Where a user has not paid remuneration, a court may prohibit the use in question until remuneration has been paid.

1. Government Bill 1996/185.

179. Section 47a provides that whenever a phonograph record or another device on which sound has been recorded has been used in a radio or television transmission which has, simultaneously and without alteration, been retransmitted, the performing artist and the producer are entitled to remuneration for the said retransmission. The remuneration may be paid only through a collecting society and must be claimed within two years counted from the end of the year during which the use took place.[1]

> 1. It should be noted that this provision does not apply to a film or any other device on which moving images have been recorded.

180. Producers' rights. Section 46 provides that a *phonograph record* or other device on which sound has been recorded may not be copied or distributed to the public without the consent of the producer. The *term of protection* is 50 years from the end of the year during which the recording took place or, where the recording has been published or disseminated within this period, 50 years from the end of the year during which the recorded performance was published or disseminated for the first time. It should be noted that all recordings enjoy protection, regardless of what has been recorded. A recording consisting of bird song enjoys protection in the same way as a recording of a symphony.

181. Section 46a provides that a *film* or other device on which moving images have been recorded may not be copied or distributed to the public without the consent of the producer. The term of protection is equal to the term of protection in the case of the rights of a producer of a record. The rights of both record and film producers are exhausted in the same way as copyright with the exception that they are subject to Community exhaustion.[1] Sections 46 and 46a are applicable where the recording or the film has been made in a Member State of the EEA.

> 1. Please *see* §7 above.

182. Radio and television transmission. Section 48 provides that a radio or television transmission may not be retransmitted or recorded without the consent of the transmitting organisation. A television transmission may not, without such consent, be made available to the public on premises to which the public has access in return for payment. Furthermore, a recorded transmission may not, without consent, be copied, retransmitted or distributed to the public until 50 years have elapsed from the year during which the first transmission took place. The rights of radio and television broadcasters are exhausted in the same way as copyright with the exception that they are subject to Community exhaustion. Section 48 is applied where the transmissions are receivable in a Member State of the EEA or where the broadcaster is domiciled in such a state.

183. Databases. Section 49 provides protection for catalogues, tables, programmes and any other productions in which large numbers of information items are compiled. In accordance with the Database Directive,[1] this protection also extends to databases which demonstrate that substantial investments have been made in obtaining, verifying or presenting the contents (*sui generis* right). The holder of the right has the exclusive right to make copies of, and make available to the public, the whole or a substantial part of the contents of the database. The term of protection is 15 years counted from the end of the year during which the database was compiled or 15 years from the end of the year in which it was made available to the public.

1. Directive of the European Parliament and of the Council of 11 March 1996 on the legal protection of databases (96/9/EC).

184. In many respects the same rules apply to databases as to computer programs. For example, they may not be copied for private use and authorship is transferred to the employer in the same way as for computer programs. It should be noted that where a database meets the requirements for a work (originality, creativity, etc.) it will also be protected by copyright.

185. Photographs. The rules on protection of photographs were recently transferred from a separate Act on Photographs[1] to Section 49a of the Copyright Act.[2] The protection conferred by the old Act on Photographs and Section 49a is in most respects similar. Photographs which meet the requirements for a work are also protected by copyright. The main differences between the right to a photograph as provided in Section 49a and copyright are in the term of protection and in the fact that the right to a photograph does not include the right to make the photograph available to the public.[3] Section 49a is applicable where the photograph has been made by a person who is a citizen of a Member State of the EEA or who is habitually domiciled in such a state.

1. Act No. 405 of 8 July 1961.
2. Act No. 446 of 23 March 1995.
3. Government Bill 1994/287 p. 55.

186. Section 49a provides that a photographer has the exclusive right, with regard to a photographic picture in a modified or unmodified form, to make copies thereof and to exhibit it publicly. All kinds of photographs are protected, including x-ray and infrared pictures, images recorded in the memory of a computer and so on. The term of protection is 50 years counted from the end of the year during which the photograph was made. The right to a photograph is exhausted in the same way as copyright.

187. Press reports. The final neighbouring right protects news. Section 50 provides that a press report supplied by a foreign press agency or by a correspondent abroad pursuant to a contract, may not be made available to the public through newspaper or radio publication without the consent of its recipient, until twelve hours have elapsed reckoned from the time of its dissemination in Finland. This does not prevent another newspaper or radio broadcaster from obtaining the same report from abroad and making it available to the public.

§10. INFRINGEMENT AND REMEDIES

188. Chapter 7 of the Copyright Act concerns penal sanctions and liability for infringements of copyright. Section 60 provides that the same provisions apply to neighbouring rights. Generally speaking, damages for copyright infringements are often sought through criminal proceedings. Interim measures are usually more difficult to obtain in civil proceedings.[1]

1. R. Hilli p. 129.

189. Penal sanctions. Wilful infringement of copyright (or of a neighbouring right) is punishable as a *copyright offence*, provided that the infringer has committed the infringement for gain and the infringement causes significant damage to the author. Also where illegally copied protected works or goods have been imported (*piracy*) and this causes considerable damage to the author, the infringer is to be punished for a copyright offence. The penalty for such an offence is a fine or a term of imprisonment not exceeding two years (Section 56 of the Copyright Act and Chapter 49, Section 1 of the Penal Code).

190. Where the infringement does not amount to a copyright offence, anyone who wilfully or out of gross negligence infringes copyright or imports into Finland a copy of a work for distribution to the public, which copy he knows or has well-founded reason to suspect to have been produced contrary to the Copyright Act is to be sentenced to pay a fine for a *copyright misdemeanour* (Sect. 56a). Sections 56b to 56d provide for certain other kinds of copyright violations. Criminal proceedings may not be brought by a public prosecutor unless the injured party has reported the infringement for the purpose of prosecution (Sect. 61).

191. Compensation and damages. Section 57, paragraph 1 provides that the author is entitled to *fair compensation* for any unauthorised use. Section 57 paragraph 2 provides that if such use is wilful or arises from negligence, then the delinquent party must, in addition to fair compensation, also pay *damages* for any other losses, together with pain and suffering and other injury. In practice it has been difficult for the delinquent party to prove that he has not acted negligently and therefore in most cases damages are ordered in addition to fair compensation.

192. The author is always entitled to *fair compensation*, regardless of whether or not the delinquent party has been negligent. Fair compensation is intended only to constitute compensation for the use of the work and comprises no elements of indemnification. In the Supreme Court judgment *SC 1968 II 81 (Tammelundin Liikenne Oy)* fair compensation was held to be twice the amount of the normal licence fees. It should be noted that this does not have the status of a general rule, even though authors often claim twice the amount of the normal licence fee as fair compensation. For example, in the judgments *SC 1989:87 (Valintatalo)* and *SC 1995:202*, both of which did not concern piracy, it was held that fair compensation was equal to the licence fees for the video cassettes concerned. In *SC 1989:151* the Supreme Court held that the fact that the delinquent party had committed piracy should influence the amount of fair compensation. Therefore, the amount of fair compensation might in practice depend on the culpability of the delinquent party.

Court of Appeal of Helsinki judgment of 11 May 1995 (Videos)
The District Court of Helsinki had held that fair compensation should be assessed on the basis of the normal licencing terms and fees. However, the Court of Appeal held that application of the normal terms and fees in the case would lead to unreasonable consequences and, therefore, the amount of fair compensation was modified.
Court of Appeal of Helsinki judgement of 3 March 1996 (Jewellery)
The defendant had continued the production and sale of jewellery items designed by the plaintiff without his consent following the termination of their initial agreement. The Court held that fair compensation was six per cent of the sale price not including VAT.

193. The author is entitled to *damages in full*, in addition to fair compensation, where the use is wilful or arises from negligence. These damages should correspond precisely to the injury suffered by the author. The injured party is entitled to damages for such injuries as reduced sales, market damages, direct losses and so on. Damages for pain and suffering and for other injuries are paid only rarely.[1] The provisions of the Act on Damages and Tort Liability are also effective with regard to damages payable in cases of this kind. It should be noted that according to a general rule of Finnish tort law, the injured party is not to be put in a better position than that in which he would have been had the injury not occurred.

1. *See* R. Oesch (1989) pp. 85–86.

194. At the request of the injured party the court may order that unauthorised copies or copies of works which have been altered in a prohibited manner, are to be *destroyed, altered or conveyed* against compensation to the injured party (Sect. 58). However, this does not apply to a party which has obtained the property or a specific right thereto in good faith.

§11. Overlapping and Relation to Other Intellectual Property Laws

195. Trademarks. Section 14, paragraph 5 of the Trademarks Act provides that a trademark may not be registered if it is composed of, or contains anything likely to give the impression of being the title of a protected literary or artistic work of another party, whenever such a work is of original character, or if it constitutes an infringement of the copyright held by another party to such a work.

196. This does not, however, prevent the registration of, for example, the title of one's own protected literary or artistic work as a trademark. More importantly, for example, a picture within a protected trademark may also obtain copyright protection as an artistic work. Thus there are no obstacles to the same subject acquiring protection at the same time both as a trademark and through copyright, provided that the necessary requirements for these protections are met.

197. Registered designs. Sometimes where artistic works such as jewellery, furniture, light fittings, shag rugs, tools or utensils do not meet the requirement for protection as works, they may obtain protection as registered designs. This is important since the requirements for these to obtain copyright protection are generally set at a fairly high level. There are no obstacles to protected works acquiring additional protection as registered designs. However, Section 4(c) provides that a design may not be registered where it contains anything that may be interpreted as the title of a protected literary or artistic work by another person, provided that the title concerned is distinctive, or if it contains anything which infringes the copyright of another party to such a work.

198. Computer programs protected by patents. In some circumstances computer programs may obtain protection both by copyright and by patent.

199. Confidentiality. Section 4 of the Unfair Trade Practices Act concerns trade secrets and confidentiality. It provides that no one may without justification obtain, or attempt to obtain, information regarding a trade secret, or use or disclose any information so obtained. Where somebody has obtained a trade secret from another knowing that the other has obtained the information without justification, he may not use or disclose such information. This provision may be applicable, for example, in the case of information held in databases, non-disseminated scientific works and so on.

200. Integrated circuits. Integrated circuits are briefly discussed in §2, II above. They are discussed more extensively in Chapter 8 under the heading of chip protection.

Chapter 2. Patents

§1. SOURCES – LEGISLATION

Bibliography in Finnish or Nordic languages:
Aro, P.-L. '*Ennakkokäyttöoikeus patentinhaltijan yksinoikeuden rajoituksena*' [The Right of Prior Use as a Limitation on the Exclusive Rights of a Patent Holder], Suomalainen lakimiesyhdistys, Vammala 1972;
Godenhielm, B., '*Uppsatser i immaterialrätt*' [Essays on Intellectual Property], Norstedt & Söners Förlag, Stockholm 1983;
Godenhielm, B., '*Om ekvivalens och annat gott*' [On Equivalence], Söderström & Co Förlag, Ekenäs 1990;
Godenhielm, B., '*Patentskyddets omfattning*' [On the Scope of Patent Protection], Juristförbundets förlag, Helsinki 1994;
Haarmann, P.-L., '*Immateriaalioikeuden oppikirja*' [A Textbook on Intellectual Property Rights] 2nd ed., Lakimiesliiton kustannus, Helsinki 1994;
Jacobson, M. & Tersmeden, E. & Törnroth, L., '*Patentlagstiftningen*' [Patent Law], P. A. Norstedt & Söners förlag, Lund 1980;
Koktvedgaard, M. & Levin, M., *Lärobok i immaterialrätt* [A Textbook of Intellectual Property Rights], Norstedts Juridik, Stockholm 1997;
Koktvedgaard, M., '*Immaterialretspositioner*' [Legal Status in Intellectual Property Law], Juristförbundets förlag, Copenhagen 1965;
Levin, M., '*ECP och nationell patenträtt särskilt vad gäller datorprogram*' [EPC and National Patent Law on Software] in NIR No. 2, 1991, pp. 197–210;
Rahnasto, I., '*Keksinnöllisyysvaatimus Suomen ja Euroopan patenttijärjestelmissä*' [The Requirement of Inventiveness in the Finnish and European Patent Systems], The Finnish AIPPI Group, Helsinki 1996;
Roitto, K., '*Förnyad nyttighetsmodellag i Finland*' [The Revised Act on Utility Models in Finland], in NIR No. 2, 1996, pp. 170–172.

Bibliography in English:
Aro, P.-L., 'A Finnish Case on Compulsory Licence', in NIR No. 1, 1985, pp. 91–98;
Bruun, N., 'The Role of the Patent System in the Protection of Intellectual Property', in NIR No. 2, 1992, pp. 205–216;
Bruun, N., 'Joint Inventors/Joint Patentees', in NIR No. 4, 1993, pp. 590–600;
Castrén, M., 'The Patentability of Biotechnological Inventions in Finland', in NIR No. 1, 1996, pp. 9–21;
Cornish, W.R., '*Intellectual Property*', 2nd ed., Sweet & Maxwell, London 1989;
Godenhielm, B., '*Employee Inventions*', Ch. 7 in Ulmer, E., Copyright and Industrial Copyright, Vol. XIV of International Encyclopedia of Comparative Law (J.C.B. Mohr, Tübingen);
Hilli, R., '*Trade marks*', Ch. 6.2 in Metaxas-Maranghidis, Intellectual Property Laws of Europe (Chansery Law Publishing, Chichester 1995), pp. 130–134;

Hilli, R. et al., 'Enforcement of Intellectual Property Rights – Procedure and Sanctions', in AIPPI Q 134A No. 4, 1996, pp. 175–180;
Nordman, E. et al., 'Enforcement of Intellectual Property Rights – Procedure and Sanctions', in AIPPI Q 134B No. 5, 1996, pp. 155–174;
Pfanner, K., 'Compulsory Licensing of Patents: Survey and Recent Trends', in NIR No. 1, 1985, pp. 1–29.

Official documents:
Government Bill 1966/101;
Government Bill 1979/139;
Government Bill 1980/139;
Government Bill 1992/215;
Government Bill 1994/103;
Government Bill 1995/161;
Government Bill 1996/254;
Nordisk utredningsserie NU 1963:6.

201. The first modern patent system in Finland was created by the Patents Decree of 1898, which harmonised the law with the 1883 Paris Convention on Industrial Property.[1] The Patents Decree of 1898 was replaced by the Patents Act of 1943. The current Patents Act[2] of 1967 came into force on 1 January 1968 as a result of Nordic co-operation during the 1960s.[3] Although the Nordic patent acts were harmonised in order to enable a system of Nordic patents to be set up, in the end no such system was ever established.[4] Nevertheless, as a result of this co-operation, the basic substantive principles came to be similar in the Nordic countries and differences of detail were rather small. The Patents Act has been greatly amended since 1967. Because the amendments which have been undertaken in various Nordic Countries in order to adapt to international developments have been largely similar, the Nordic patent acts are still quite well harmonised.[5]

1. At that time Finland was part of Russia.
2. Patents Act No. 550 of 15 December 1967, last amended by the Act No. 243 of 21 March 1997.
3. Finland, Sweden, Norway and Denmark participated jointly in the preparation of the Acts. This co-operation resulted in a joint committee report, NU 1963:6.
4. In the system of Nordic patents one application would have given protection in all the Nordic countries.
5. B. Godenhielm (1990) pp. 151*ff.*

202. The Patent Co-operation Treaty (PCT) of 1970 came into force in Finland in 1980 and its implementation brought important changes in the Patents Act.[1] At the same time, the Patents Act was harmonised with the principles of the 1973 European Patent Convention (EPC). Even though the EPC came into force in Finland as late as 1 March 1996,[2] Finnish substantive patent law has, with some minor exceptions, fulfilled the requirements of the EPC since 1980. The Patents Act has also been recently harmonised with the TRIPS agreement.[3]

1. Act No. 407 of 6 June 1980. Government Bill 1979/139.
2. Act No. 1695 of 22 December 1995. Government Bill 1995/161.
3. Agreement on Trade-Related Aspects of Intellectual Property Rights.

Patents, Ch. 2

203. Besides the Patents Act and Patents Decree, important sources of law are the judgments of the Supreme Court (SC), the Supreme Administrative Court (SAC) and the Court of Appeal of Helsinki. In several areas, however, there is rather little case law. The decisions of the Board of Appeal of the National Board of Patents and Registration (the Patent Office) are therefore the main sources concerning the interpretation in practice of the Patents Act. The Patent Regulations of the Patent Office are also important.

§2. PATENTABLE SUBJECT MATTER

204. The two main requirements for patents are provided in Section 1, paragraph 1 of the Patents Act: only *inventions* may be patented and the inventions must be *capable of industrial application*. Furthermore, the invention must be replicable. 'Invention' is not defined in the Patents Act and therefore the provision is not very helpful in defining patentable subject matter. Section 1, paragraphs 2 and 3 provide, however, some restrictions as to what may be regarded as inventions.

205. Invention. An invention must be of *technical character*, which excludes discoveries and 'pure expressions of human intelligence'. A discovery is not an invention that constructs something new, it merely reveals something that already exists. A discovery is the unearthing of causes, properties or phenomena already existing in nature, whereas an invention is the application of such knowledge.[1]

1. W.R. Cornish p. 139.

206. It is quite easy to distinguish between discoveries and inventions in traditional areas of industry, such as mechanical engineering and electronics. However, the line between discoveries and inventions can be blurred and is not always clear in modern technologies, e.g. inventions concerning chemical compounds and microbiology. In principle the traditional rule is still valid, but the scope of patentable subject matter is becoming broader. For example, whereas substances freely existing in nature may not be patented, the process of isolating and obtaining them from the surroundings may be patentable. Even though substances may exist in nature, they may be patentable provided that they are made available for the first time and in a well defined form.

207. Section 1, paragraph 2 gives examples of what are not regarded as inventions and thus are not patentable. It provides that discoveries, scientific theories, mathematical methods, aesthetic creations, schemes, rules and methods for performing mental acts, playing games or doing business, computer programs and the presentation of information are not as such to be regarded as inventions. A subject matter which is not patentable may, however, obtain protection through copyright or other intellectual property rights.

208. Inventions shall, when possible, relate to one of the following categories: products, apparatus, processes or use.[1] The possibility of patenting inventions in various categories is especially important for inventions concerning chemical compounds and pharmaceuticals. Where a chemical compound or a pharmaceutical is protected by a *product patent*, the exploitation of the substance itself is protected. Generally the principle of unlimited (absolute) product protection is also applied to chemical compounds.[2] The protected substance is described by its chemical formula or name and by describing its chemical and physical properties. In such a case the chemical compound must be new as such, but practice concerning what is considered as new varies between different countries.[3]

1. Section 14, para. 3 of the Patents Decree.
2. Until the Patents Act was amended in 1985 (Sect. 8, para. 2), product protection for chemical compounds was limited to the specific use disclosed.
3. M. Koktvedgaard & M. Levin p. 204.

209. The process or method of manufacturing a certain substance is patented by means of a *process patent*. For a process patent, the process of manufacturing must be new, whereas e.g. the chemical compound need not be. Where a chemical compound is not patentable as such because, for example, of lack of novelty, the process of isolating it may be patentable. Moreover, many chemical compounds can be manufactured in several different ways and the invention may concern a new, better or cheaper way to manufacture them. A *use patent* applies in cases where a certain use of a chemical compound is patented. In such a case, the substance is used in a different way or for a different purpose from those which have been known earlier. As with product patents, the substance does not have to be new, but it must be used in a different way.

210. Pharmaceutical and biotechnological inventions are patentable on basically the same grounds as chemical compounds and the patents can be divided into the same categories.[1] However, the therapeutic effects of a pharmaceutical must be disclosed in the patent. Section 1, paragraph 3 excludes from patentable subject matter methods for surgical or therapeutic treatment or diagnostic methods. Products, substances and compositions for use in such methods may, however, be patented.

1. M. Koktvedgaard & M. Levin pp. 199*ff.*

211. Section 1, paragraph 4(2) provides that plant or animal varieties or essentially biological processes for the production thereof may not be patented. Essentially biological processes are normally based on traditional, natural hybridisation, selective breeding or some other kind of regeneration. However, where a new plant has been obtained through a microbiological process, the process and the products resulting from that process may be patented.

212. In Finland and Sweden processes for genetic engineering [gene manipulation], have generally been regarded as patentable.[1] The practice and opinions of the EPO concerning the patentability of plants and animal varieties, as well as of biological and microbiological processes, have had an impact on prevailing opinion in this matter. There is no further legislation as yet in this area, but the Government has stated that it is waiting for the European Parliament and Council Directive on the legal protection of biotechnical inventions.

1. The practice in Norway and Denmark has been more restrictive on this point.

213. Patents cannot be granted for inventions that would be *contrary to morality or public policy* (Section 1, paragraph 4(1)). Some inventions concerning plant and animal varieties, as well as biological and microbiological processes, might be considered to be contrary to public policy or morality and, therefore, not patentable. For example, inventions concerning the human body or parts of the human body and the process of modifying the genetic identity of the human body are most likely not patentable. Moreover, the process of modifying the genetic identity of animals may be non-patentable.[1]

   1. M. Castrén (1996) pp. 12*ff.*

214. It should also be noted that in some circumstances certain elements of *computer programs* might also be protected by patents in addition to copyright protection. Firstly, a program may be included as an element of a process patent, e.g. in inventions where the technical effect is obtained by using a program.[1] Secondly, a program may be included in a patent of computer hardware. Thus, it is possible that computer programs may in some circumstances obtain protection through both copyright and patent.[2]

   1. *See* e.g. M. Levin, in NIR No. 2, 1991, pp. 197–210.
   2. M. Koktvedgaard & M. Levin p. 197.

215. Capability of industrial application. The invention must be capable of industrial application. 'Industrial' is broadly defined and includes not only industry in a strict sense, but also other areas of the economy such as transport, construction, agriculture, fisheries, handicrafts, etc. The invention must be eligible for use in practice. Inventions of no practical use are not patentable, but the requirements for usefulness are low, e.g. toys etc. meet the requirements of practical use. Products of scientific research are not patentable as such if there is no industrially applicable invention. In a decision of 1989, the Board of Appeal of the Patent Office held that a certain application is concerned more with a product of scientific research than an industrially applicable invention.[1] The invention must be capable of industrial application at the time of filing the application documents.

   1. Decision issued on 20 December 1989 by the Board of Appeal of the Patent Office, appeal reg. No. 75/P/86.

216. Technical effect. It is also required that an invention has technical effect. This simply means that it leads to the desired outcome and it works as it should. Even though the inventive step is a requirement for patentability, it is not required that the invention leads to technological progress or improvement. However, the invention must solve the problem or fulfil the purpose for which it was designed. The effect of the invention and the description of the invention must be clear enough for a person skilled in the art to be able to use the invention and to bring about the claimed result.

217. Replicability. Finally, the invention must be *replicable*, meaning that it must be capable of repetition so that the desired effect is obtained. This requirement is important mainly for inventions concerning gene technology. The inventor does not need to be able to give a scientific explanation for the invention, but he must describe the invention clearly enough that a person skilled in the art is able to use the invention based on the description.

§3. Conditions of Patentability

218. Finnish patent law stipulates two conditions for an invention to be patentable. These are *novelty and inventive step*.[1] The requirements are set out in Section 2, which states that: 'Patents may be granted only for inventions which are new in relation to what was known before the filing date of the patent application and which also differ essentially therefrom.' It is important to note that the requirements are to be considered separately. The Nordic Patent Acts are also harmonised to a large extent with regard to conditions for patentability and thus the practice of the courts of the other Nordic countries may also have some relevance in Finland.

> 1. Some authors regard technical effect to be a third requirement for patentability.

219. Novelty. Section 2, paragraph 2 provides that everything which has been made available to the public in writing, in lectures, through public use or otherwise shall be considered to be known. This means that the novelty must be absolute and objective. Objective novelty, contrary to subjective novelty, means that an invention that is new only to the inventor, but known to someone else, is not considered to be new. Absolute novelty means that wherever, whenever and however the invention has become available to the public, it is not considered as new anymore and is thus not patentable. An invention that already forms a part of the state of the art is not patentable because it is not new.

220. An invention may become publicly available *inter alia* through books, journals, articles, earlier patent applications, in lectures, through use, etc., i.e. in any form in writing, orally, through use or in any other way. In practice the most important obstacles to novelty are prior applications in any country.[1]

Patent Office decision of 28 February 1995 (Adram SNC)
The Board of Appeal held that an EP application had become available to the public on the date which was on the cover of the publication EP 04022252 and was marked as the date of the Inid 43-code.

> 1. In practice the Patent Office mainly examines EP and PCT applications, and to some extent those made in the most important trading partners of Finland. Where necessary, other sources may also be examined.

221. Particularly in cases where an invention has been exploited prior to the application date, the question of whether it has been made available to the public may arise. Normally, if the invention has been used only within a company, it is not considered to be publicly available. However, if it has been used for a long time and many employees know about it, then it might be considered to be available to the public. There is also a lack of novelty where the invention is used in places to which the public has free access or where products incorporating the invention are sold.

Supreme Court (SC) 1988:16 (Pipette)
The applicant had sold 45 pipettes incorporating the invention, before the date of application and without any secrecy concluded an agreement with the buyer concerning the invention. Thus, an unspecified number of people had had the opportunity to learn of the invention and it had become available to the public before the date of application.
Patent Office decision 260/P/93 of 28 November 1995 (Eka Nobel Ab)
The application for a process patent was rejected by the Board of Appeal because the process had been used in three factories of an opponent for several years before the application.

222. Nowadays the examination of novelty is quite formal. The Finnish Patent Office pays no attention to equivalents etc. Inventions are considered to lack novelty only when a person skilled in the art considers them to be identical [or almost identical] to prior inventions. This person shall have regard only to the material presented and shall make no extensive studies. A more extensive examination is made when considering the requirement for inventive step. The distinction between novelty and inventive step is, however, not always clear.[1]

Court of Appeal judgment S 95/1808 of 17 December 1996 (AWA Oy)
The Court held that elements from different sources and documents may not be combined when judging the novelty of a patent, whereas such combination shall be performed when evaluating the inventive step.

1. M. Koktvedgaard & M. Levin pp. 219–220.

223. As in most other countries, the *first-to-file* principle is applicable in Finland. This means that if many persons have made the same invention, then the one who first files an application for a patent with the Patent Office is awarded the patent for the invention, irrespective of who was first to make the invention.

224. *Exceptions to the requirement of novelty.*[1] Two applications that are similar or related to the same invention may each be filed within a short period of time. Since the first application does not become publicly available immediately, it does not affect the novelty of the second application. However, if the first application is accepted or becomes public in accordance with Section 22, then it becomes *retroactively* a restraint on the novelty of the second application (Section 2, para. 2). Provided that novelty exists, the first application does not affect the inventive step of the second application, even after it has become publicly available.

1. Even though there are some exceptions to the requirement of novelty, there is no actual *grace period* in Finland.

225. In the very unusual case that two applications concerning the same invention are filed on the same day, both may obtain the patent. A joint ownership is

thereby constituted.[1] Furthermore, if another person was commercially exploiting the invention at the time of the application, then he may continue to do so notwithstanding the issuing of the patent. Such a right of prior use may also be claimed by a person who has made substantial preparations for commercial exploitation of the invention.[2] The right can be transferred to another party only together with the business in which it originated or in which the exploitation was intended to take place (Sect. 4).

1. Joint ownership is not governed by patent legislation, but by general private [civil] law.
2. Note, however, that if the invention is considered to have become public through its use by the other party, there is lack of novelty and the patent cannot be granted at all. Compare this with judgment No. 260/P/93 of the Board of Appeal of the Patent Office of 28 November 1995 (Eka Nobel Ab).

226. The most important exception to this is *convention priority*, which is an important rule in international patent co-operation. Section 6 provides that an inventor has the right to apply for a patent in Finland within 12 months reckoned from the date of the first application for a patent on the same invention in another country which is a member of the convention.[1] Upon request, the application in Finland is deemed to have been made on the same date as the first application when assessing prior art and prior use. In practice, convention priority leads to a longer period of protection because the invention is protected from the date of the first application, whereas the 20-year period of protection is counted from the date of filing the application in Finland.[2]

1. The Paris Convention for the Protection of Industrial Property or the Agreement Establishing the World Trade Organisation.
2. M. Koktvedgaard & M. Levin pp. 223–224.

227. Section 2, paragraph 4 provides that patents may be granted for known substances or compositions for use in surgical, therapeutic or diagnostic methods, provided that the use of the substance or composition is not known in such a method.

228. Section 2, paragraph 5 provides that patents may be granted even though the invention has been made available to the public, if the disclosure was a result of an *evident abuse*, e.g. industrial espionage, abuse of a confidential relationship, etc., or the invention has been displayed at certain *international exhibitions*. In such cases the application must be filed within six months of the disclosure.

229. *Inventive step*.[1] Section 2, paragraph 1 also requires that a patentable invention *differs essentially* from the prior art and thus no patent will be granted if the invention does not differ sufficiently from earlier inventions. The importance of harmonising Finnish patent law with international and European conventions was stressed in the Government Bill for the amendments of 1980.[2] It has therefore been claimed that there are no grounds for applying the requirement of inventive step differently from, for example, its application in the EPC.[3] The EPO Guidelines might therefore serve as a guide in interpreting the Finnish Patents Act in this respect.

1. Inventive step is also called non-obviousness.
2. Government Bill 1979/139.
3. B. Godenhielm (1990) p. 17.

230. For an invention to differ essentially from the prior art, the objective difference between the invention and the state of the art must be adequate. When assessing the requirement a hypothetical *person skilled in the art* is used. The invention must not be obvious to a person skilled in the art. Unlike the assessment of novelty, the person skilled in the art shall pay regard not only to the presented material, but he shall make more extensive studies, use his knowledge, etc., in order to assess whether he would have achieved the invention. Only information and knowledge that was available at the time of filing the application may be regarded. In special cases objective criteria, such as technical progress, the overcoming of a prejudice or even economic success, may also indicate that the invention differs essentially from earlier ones.[1]

1. I. Rahnasto pp. 118*ff.* However, compare this with the following Swedish case, which would probably have been decided similarly in Finland.
Svea Court of Appeal judgment of 13 February 1991
With reference to the information that was available through a prior patent and references to literature, the invention was considered to be obvious to a person skilled in the art. The fact that the invention brought technological progress and was economically successful was disregarded. The invention lacked inventive step.

231. Even though technical progress is traditionally not required, it often helps in showing the inventive step. The courts are commonly felt to judge the requirement of inventive step more strictly than the patent authorities.[1] In some fields, such as the chemical industry, the requirement of inventive step is difficult to apply, and therefore the demands for the inventive step are not set at a particularly high level.

1. P.-L. Haarmann p. 98.

232. In *combination inventions* two or more previously known features are combined so that a new technical effect is obtained. Basically these inventions are regarded as new inventions, but there are some special characteristics. The new technical effect must meet the usual requirement for inventive step. There is no inventive step if the combined effect is only the sum of the effects of the earlier features and the effect of the combination was obvious to a person skilled in the art. Normally, 'unexpected effects' are in some degree required.

Patent Office decision 200/P/94 of 13 March 1996 (Gesertek Oy)
The Board of Appeal accepted an application for a process for manufacturing noise barriers on site. Even though the process was as such known before, the application of the process to noise barriers was unknown and furthermore, the process of manufacturing them had not been applied to manufacturing on the construction site. Since the invention was not a combination of previously known features that would have been obvious for a person skilled in the art, the invention contained an inventive step.

233. Section 2, paragraph 2 provides an exception to the requirement of inventive step. A later application is not required to have an inventive step compared to any earlier applications that become available to the public after the filing date of the later application.

§4. Formalities (Procedures for Issuing and Obtaining Patent Protection)

234. Patents are obtained through a strictly formal procedure and are granted in Finland by the National Board of Patents and Registration (the Patent Office). Since the application regulations are quite complex it is normal practice to use a patent agent. An applicant who is not domiciled in Finland must appoint a *patent agent*, domiciled in Finland, to represent him in all matters concerning the application (Sect. 12). There is a separate Act on Patent Agents[1] which regulates, *inter alia*, the authorisation and competence of patent agents. Only authorised patent agents may serve as professional patent agents or use a similar title.

1. Patent Agents Act No. 552 of 15 December 1967.

235. The application. The application must be made in writing, preferably using a form provided by the Patent Office. A description, any illustrations, the claims and the abstract must be attached to the application. The application must be submitted in the Finnish or Swedish language,[1] but if the abstract and claims are in one only of the two languages, they are to be translated to the other at the applicant's expense. However, where the applicant is not domiciled in Finland the description must be in Finnish and the abstract and claims in both languages (Sect. 8, para. 5).

1. Finnish and Swedish are the two official languages of Finland.

236. The application must include a concise and factual title for the invention and a description of the invention, one or more claims and an abstract. The name of the inventor must be stated and, where the applicant is not the inventor, he is required to prove his title to the invention (Sect. 8, para. 4). The inventor must be a natural person, whereas the applicant may also be a legal person. Sections 1–4 of the Patents Decree provide further details on applications.

237. The claims. The applicant defines the subject matter of the patent protection in the claims (Sect. 8, para. 2). Section 39 provides that the scope of protection conferred by a patent is to be determined by the claims.

238. Each claim may relate to one invention only, but many claims may be included in one application, in which case they may be independent or dependent claims. Where several independent claims are included, these should be technically connected to one another and should be based on the same single inventive concept. A dependent claim relates to an embodiment of the invention disclosed in one or many preceding claims in the application and comprises all the features of these. It states, in relation to the preceding claims, additional features characterising the invention (Sect. 15 of the Patents Decree). The claims may relate to different

Patents, Ch. 2

categories of the invention defined in the form of a product, apparatus, process and/or use.

239. In the claims, the applicant defines and clarifies the main features of the invention. The claim must contain all the essential and new elements comprising the invention. The claims also distinguish the invention concerned from other inventions, and they specify what is new in relation to other inventions as well as the elements for which the applicant seeks protection.

240. Section 14 of the Patents Decree provides that the claims shall contain (1) the title of the invention, (2) where necessary, a statement specifying the prior art [the art in relation to which the invention is new] (the introduction) and (3) a statement of the new and characteristic features of the invention (the characterising part).

241. In the *introduction* to the claim the applicant must include all the features of the invention which are necessary to define the invention but are part of the prior art. The invention will be evaluated in relation to the prior art disclosed in the introduction.[1] The introduction is usually drafted on the basis of the closest prior art document.

1. B. Godenhielm (1990) pp. 18*ff.*

242. The characterising part contains the essential features of the invention, which are new in relation to the prior art. The difference in relation to the prior art should be substantial, so that the invention as a whole meets the requirement of inventive step. Normally, the claims contain mainly technical information. However, functional features are also allowed. The introduction part and the characterising part are separated by the words 'characterised in that'.[1]

1. In Finnish: 'tunnettu siitä', and in Swedish: 'kännetecknad av'.

243. Section 39 provides that the claims determine the scope of the protection whereas the description serves as a guideline in interpreting the claims. In Finnish patent law the claims, with the description as guideline, were intended to be strictly interpreted.[1] However, actual practice shows that Finnish courts also consider other aspects such as the prior art and the correspondence between the applicant and the Patent Office.[2] The interpretation of claims and extent of protection are further discussed below in Section 6 dealing with exclusive rights.

1. B. Godenhielm (1994) p. 217.
2. Compare this, however, with M. Koktvedgaard & M. Levin p. 244.

244. Section 13 provides that an application for a patent may not be amended in such a way as to claim protection for a matter not disclosed in the application at the time it was filed. Similarly, Section 19 of the Patents Decree provides that claims may not be amended to include any subject matter not disclosed in a document constituting a basic document. It has been held that these provisions mean that, for example, marginal values may not be limited.[1] However, the following SAC decision might have changed this view.

SAC decision 844/4/95 of 13 February 1996 (Hollming Oy)
The applicant had amended the claims to include a marginal value of 20–50 per cent instead of the original value of 20–60 per cent, even though the value of 50 per cent had not been stated in the original documents. The SAC considered that the amendment was not prohibited by Section 13 and approved the application.

    1. E.g. NU 1963:6, p. 199.

245. The description. The description is central to the patent system. Its purpose is to disclose the invention to others and thus to promote technological progress. The description, together with necessary illustrations, must be sufficiently clear to enable a person skilled in the art to duplicate the invention. However, the description may contain only subject matter that assists in understanding the invention. Section 39 provides that the description may serve as guidance in interpreting the claims.

246. The description is divided into a general part and a special part. The general part must contain information about the field of application of the invention and information about the technology on which the invention is based, i.e. the state of the art. The applicant must make references to any literature and documents known to him which disclose the state of the art. The applicant must also point out what is achieved by the invention in relation to the state of the art and the means required for it. The special part must contain a thorough explanation of the invention, e.g. by giving examples of its use. The examples must support and illustrate the claims. When necessary references must be made to illustrations.[1]

Patent Office[2] decision of 24 May 1995 (Biohit Oy)
The applicant had not adequately described the state of the art. It was not clear from the description how the process of the invention differed from what had earlier been known, and what significance the differences had for such aspects as the speed and accuracy of the process. The invention was therefore considered to lack inventive step and the application was rejected.

    1. B. Godenhielm (1994) p. 116, Patent regulations Sects. 5–6.
    2. The Board of Appeal of the Patent Office.

247. The patent system is based on written descriptions clarified with illustrations. Chemical formulae are generally included in applications for chemical inventions. However, Section 8a provides that if the invention relates to a microbiological process or a product thereof, and it is not possible to provide a clear description, then a culture of the micro-organism involved in the invention shall be deposited. The deposition is to be made in accordance with the Budapest Treaty.[1] Sections 17a–17c of the Patents Decree provide further details concerning the manner in which a deposit is to be made.

    1. Treaty on the International Recognition of the Deposit of Micro-organisms for the Purposes of Patent Procedure of 28 April 1977.

248. The abstract. The abstract must be based on the description and the claims.

Patents, Ch. 2 249 – 253

It must disclose the technical problem to which the invention relates, the principles of the solution and the primary field in which the invention is to be used (Sect. 18 of the Patents Decree). It may be a maximum of 150 words in length and may also contain a picture. Section 8, paragraph 3 provides that the abstract shall merely serve for use as technical information and may not be considered for any other purpose. This means that it is of no significance for the scope of protection.

249. The procedure. Applications for patents are filed at the Patent Office in writing and using a standard form. As explained above, the application must contain a description, illustrations where necessary, one or more claims and an abstract. Where the applicant wants to enjoy *priority* based on an earlier application, he must claim such priority within three months of the date of the application (Sect. 10 of the Patents Decree).

250. The applicant must pay the prescribed *application fee* at the time of filing application.[1] A patent may not be sought in the same application in respect of two or more inventions that are independent of one another (Sect. 10).

1. The application fee was FIM 1,200 on 1 July 1997.

251. The procedure in the Patent Office begins with a *formal examination* of the *requirements* for the application. The Patent Office checks that the application contains the necessary information and documentation about the applicant and the inventor, the applicant's title to the invention, the patent agent, etc. If the applicant fails to satisfy the requirements, then the Patent Office issues an official notice to this effect.

252. After the formal examination, the Patent Office examines whether the application meets the other requirements for patentability, such as novelty and inventive step.[1] During the *examination* there is often a considerable correspondence or 'discussion' between the Patent Office and the applicant, during which the Patent Office may issue several official notices. The Patent Office may order the applicant to correct or specify the description or the claims so that the application meets the requirements. The applicant may restrict the claims during the proceedings, but they may not be amended to include subject matter not disclosed in the basic documents.

1. The Patent Office examines novelty with regard to earlier applications made in the most important trading partners of Finland and other available literature (Sect. 26 of the Patents Decree).

253. Paragraphs 2 and 3 of Section 15 provide that if an applicant fails to file observations or take steps to change the application within the prescribed time period, then the application is to be *dismissed*. If the applicant files the required response and pays a reinstatement fee within four months, then the application may be *reinstated*. If, after filing the observations, there still remains an obstacle to approval upon which the applicant has had an opportunity to comment, then the application must be *rejected* (Sect. 16). Where *another party claims proper title* to the invention, the Patent Office may invite him to institute legal proceedings within a prescribed period, failing which the claim may be disregarded in the further proceedings. The application may be suspended until the final decision is issued by the court (Sect. 17). If the other person proves that he has proper title, then the application shall be transferred to him upon request. The application may not be dismissed, rejected or granted until a final decision has been taken on the request (Sect. 18).

254. When the Patent Office has examined the application, and if it satisfies the formal requirements and no obstacles are found, then the applicant is to be notified that the *application can be accepted.* The Patent Office must approve the application after the applicant has paid the printing fee, which is to be paid within two months of the notice. The patent is granted on the day on which approval is announced (Sects. 19 and 20).

255. Where a patent has been granted, any person may file an *opposition* to the patent within nine months of the date of issuing of the patent.[1] The Patent Office must revoke the patent due to the opposition if the patent does not meet the necessary requirements. However, the patentee is given an opportunity to submit observations on the opposition. He may also amend the patent during the proceedings and, where there are no longer any obstacles to awarding the patent, it shall be maintained in the amended form. In such a case, the patentee shall pay a fee for reprinting the patent within two months of the decision. In certain circumstances, the Patent Office may consider the opposition even if the patent has lapsed or the opposition is withdrawn (Sects. 24 and 25).

1. Before 1 April 1997 oppositions were to be filed before the issuing of the patent and after the Patent Office had made the application open for inspection.

256. A final decision of the Patent Office may be *appealed* by the applicant if the decision has not been in his favour. A patentee or opposer may similarly appeal against an adverse decision arising from an opposition. An appeal may be examined even if it has been withdrawn (Sect. 26). The appeal is to be filed with the Board of Appeal of the Patent Office within 60 days of the date on which the appellant was informed of the decision and a prescribed fee is to be paid within the same time limit.[1] The decision of the Board of Appeal is further appealable to the Supreme Administrative Court within 60 days of the date on which the appellant was informed of the decision (Sect. 27). No administrative re-examination of a patent which has been granted is possible in Finland.

1. It might be noted that the Board of Appeal is a part of the Patent Office, i.e. it is not completely independent of the registration authority.

257. Division and separation. Where more than one invention has been disclosed in the basic documents, the applicant may divide the application into two or more applications as provided in Section 22 of the Patents Decree. Where the application has been amended to disclose an invention that was not disclosed in the basic documents, a new application may be separated from the original application (Section 23 of the Patents Decree).

258. Publicity of documents. The documents pertaining to a patent shall be available to the public as from the date on which the patent was issued. However, irrespective of whether the patent has been issued, the documents shall become public 18 months after the filing date of the application or the priority date, provided that the application is still pending. At the request of the applicant, the documents may also be made available earlier (Section 22). Where the documents have become available to the public before the issuing of the patent, the abstract shall be printed as soon as possible.

259. Section 56, paragraph 1 provides that an applicant who invokes his patent application against another person before the documents have become public as provided in Section 22 is required to allow such person access to the documents.

§5. Ownership and Transfer (Assignment – Licences)

260. Ownership. The inventor or his successor in title is entitled to apply for a patent (Sect. 1). It is a generally accepted principle that the original right to an invention is always held by *one or several individuals*, the inventor or inventors.[1] Nordic legislation does not recognise so-called corporate inventions. A legal person can acquire derived patent rights only.[2] An assignment document signed by the inventor(s) is required by the Patent Office to prove entitlement.

1. The Nordic patent law differs in this respect from, for example, Anglo-Saxon law.
2. N. Bruun (1993) pp. 590*ff.*

261. Section 17 provides that where it is not clear who has the right to the invention, the matter may be decided by the court. Section 18 provides that if another party proves that he has proper title to the invention, then the patent application is to be transferred to him.

262. Where a person has made an invention independently, the right to the invention is held by him, unless the rights have been transferred to another person. Where two or more persons have made the same invention independently of one another, the *first to file* the application will obtain the patent rights.

263. However, it is not completely clear what the situation is when *several persons have jointly made an invention*.[1] Normally, where it is not appropriate for each party to have the right to his own specific part of the invention, the inventors shall hold the invention jointly, in which case the general provisions on joint proprietorship may be applied analogously.[2] One general principle is that joint inventors may dispose of the invention only together, which requires them to agree in all essential respects on how to use their invention.[3] The parties are free to agree on how they arrange the ownership.

Court of Appeal judgment of 20 June 1996 (Paakkanen)
The proprietor of the patent (Puumalainen), while working as a consultant in a project for a company, had co-operated with the plaintiff (Paakkanen), who was

employed by the company. The Court considered that the invention was a result of this co-operation. Therefore, the Court held that Puumalainen and Paakkanen were jointly to be considered as the inventors.

1. The application must contain the name of all of the inventors.
2. The provisions of the Copyright Act concerning joint proprietorship cannot be directly applied to patents.
3. N. Bruun (1993) pp. 590–592.

264. Employee inventions. Inventions are more and more often made in companies, which leads to some problems concerning the ownership of rights to the inventions and of remuneration for them. The *Act on the Rights to Employee Inventions*[1] governs ownership and remuneration where inventions are made within employment relationships.

1. Act on the Rights to Employee Inventions No. 656 of 29 December 1967 (as amended).

265. The Act applies to inventions made by employees engaged either in private or public employment, irrespective of the status or level of the employee or of the duration of the employment.[1] However, the Act is not applicable to teachers and other persons conducting research at universities or equivalent institutions. Furthermore, the Act applies only to inventions which are patentable in Finland, but it is not required in order for the Act to apply that a patent is actually sought, nor that it is issued. It is presumed that an invention is patentable where the rights of the employee to seek a patent for the invention are restricted and transferred to the employer. Most provisions of the Act are non-mandatory, but the most important employee rights are mandatory.

1. B. Godenhielm (Employee Inventions) p. 18.

266. All employees have a similar initial right of ownership of an invention (obligatory provision). Employer rights are always derived from the employee rights to the invention, i.e. the Act does not recognise corporate inventions. However, an employer is, in certain circumstances, entitled to *acquire all rights to an invention* in return for reasonable remuneration. This is the case where the invention is made as a result of the employee's activity in fulfilling his professional duties or when the invention is made substantially through the application of experience gained in the employer's enterprise, provided that the invention falls within the employer's actual field of activities. Also, if the invention is made as a result of a detailed assignment or commission given to the employee in the course of the employment, then the employer is entitled to such rights even though the invention does not lie within the employer's field of activities.

267. The employer acquires *the right to exploit the invention* where the invention falls within the employer's field of activities, but is made in some other (looser) employment relationship as provided above. Finally, the *employee is obliged to offer the rights to the employer* before he offers them to another party if the employer wishes to acquire broader rights than the right to exploit the invention or if he wishes to acquire the rights to an invention falling within his field of activities, but which has been made outside of the employment relationship.

268. The employee is obliged to notify the employer when he has made a patentable invention to which the employer may acquire rights as explained. The employer, in turn, is obliged to inform the inventor within four months of such a notice, whether he will exercise his rights.

269. The employee has the right to reasonable remuneration in compensation for the rights transferred to the employer (mandatory provision). The parties may not otherwise agree before the invention is made. However, it is possible to agree on the remuneration afterwards.[1] In fixing the remuneration consideration shall be given to the value of the invention, to the scope of the rights which the employer acquires, to the terms of the employment and to the significance which the employment may have had in the making of the invention.

Court of Appeal judgment of 2 May 1996 (Besta Oy)
The inventor had agreed with his employer (Meira Oy) on remuneration for an invention to be paid as a lump sum. Meira Oy had transferred its business with all rights and obligations, including the patent for the invention, to Besta Oy. The Court held that by the lump-sum settlement with Meira Oy, the inventor had transferred to Meira Oy all his rights to the patent, including future rights, and that Meira Oy was free to transfer the rights it had thus obtained. Therefore, and since conditions had not substantially changed, the inventor was entitled to no further remuneration.

1. The provisions of such an agreement may later be adjusted by a court if they are considered to be unreasonable or unjustified.

270. The Employee Inventions Board issues non-binding advisory opinions in cases concerning employee inventions. The members of the Board represent the Government, the employer associations, the trade unions and inventors. Both the employer and the employee, as well as a court and the Patent Office, may request an advisory opinion. Where agreed by the parties, the Board may also serve as a Court of Arbitration. The Government meets the expenses of the Board although the applicant pays an opinion fee.

271. Transfer of ownership. The right to seek a patent for an invention, the patent application and the patent itself are freely transferable. The inventor may agree to transfer his rights to an invention or future inventions to another person. General contractual rules apply to such agreements. Registration is not compulsory but it makes the transfer enforceable against third parties. Patent rights may be transferred in execution and bankruptcy proceedings or by expropriation.[1] A patent and patent application may be mortgaged. There are no formal requirements for such a mortgage.

1. M. Jacobson & E. Tersmeden & L. Törnroth p. 42. However, *see also* M. Koktvedgaard & M. Levin pp. 229–230.

272. By *licencing* the patent, the proprietor may assign to another the right to use the patent. The licence may be either exclusive or non-exclusive. Section 43 provides that a licensee has no right to sub-licence the patent to a third party without the consent of the proprietor. A licensee may bring an action before the court independently from the proprietor (Sects. 63 and 64).[1] The parties are free to determine the terms of the licencing agreement, but it should be noted that certain provisions of exclusive licences might be prohibited by Sections 4–9 of the Act on Restriction of Competition[2] or Articles 85 or 86 of the Treaty of Rome.

1. P.-L. Haarmann p. 115.
2. Act on Restrictions on Competition No. 480 of 27 May 1992.

273. Registration of a transfer of patent, the issuing of a licence or the mortgaging of a patent is not compulsory and does not affect the relation between the parties, but it has some important consequences in third party relations. Section 44, paragraph 4 provides that the person last recorded in the register as the patentee shall be deemed the proprietor for the purposes of lawsuits and for other matters pertaining to the patent.

274. Where a patent has been granted to a person other than the person entitled to it under Section 1, the court must transfer the patent to the latter party (Sect. 53, para. 1). Proceedings to transfer the patent to the right person must be initiated by the person himself within one year of learning of the patent. However, where the proprietor acted in good faith at the time the patent was granted or assigned to him, proceedings may not be instituted later than three years after the date of issue of the patent (Sect. 52, para. 4). Furthermore, if the person deprived of the patent acted in good faith and began commercial exploitation, or made substantial preparations for doing so, then he is entitled to continue the exploitation on reasonable terms (Sect. 53, para. 2). Such rights may be transferred only together with the business in which they are exploited.

§6. Scope of Exclusive Rights

275. Exclusive rights. The proprietor of a patent has the exclusive right to the *commercial exploitation of the invention*. The content of this right is expressed in Section 3, which defines the rights negatively. It means that the proprietor is not regarded as having any absolute rights to exploit the invention, but may only prohibit others from doing so. Thus, if the invention is dependent on another patent or the use of the invention is prohibited by other legislation, then the proprietor cannot exploit the patent.[1]

1. However, the proprietor might get a compulsory licence for a patent which is necessary for the dependent patent (Sect. 46).

276. The proprietor may give his consent to another person to exploit the patent. Consent is normally given in a licencing agreement, but it should be noted that it may also be given with no explicit agreement, e.g. permission to import protected products is considered, if not otherwise agreed, to include permission to sell the said goods.

Patents, Ch. 2

277. The exclusive rights are national, i.e. the patent rights to a Finnish patent are in force only on Finnish territory. Ships and aircraft under the Finnish flag are regarded as Finnish territory.[1]

1. M. Jacobson & E. Tersmeden & L. Törnroth p. 106.

278. The protection provided in Section 3 may be divided into *product protection, process protection and indirect product protection*. The exploitation of a patent without the consent of the proprietor is prohibited as *direct infringement* when the infringer himself exploits the patent. Assisting someone else in infringing a patent is called *contributory infringement* and is also prohibited.

279. Before the amendments of 1980, Section 3 contained a general prohibition on exploiting a patent which belongs to another person. In order to harmonise the Patent Act with the EPC, Section 3 was amended so that the general prohibition was replaced by a detailed list of forms of exploitation that are included in the exclusive right. However, it is generally considered that the detailed list contains all forms of exploitation that would have been prohibited by the earlier general prohibition.[1]

1. M. Jacobson & E. Tersmeden & L. Törnroth p. 102.

280. A product protected by a patent may not be manufactured, offered, put on the market, or used, imported or possessed for these purposes (Sect. 3, subpara. 1) (*product patent*). 'Put on the market' includes selling, renting, lending, etc., and for a product to be put on the market it is not necessary that the product is actually sold etc., but it is sufficient that steps to put the product on the market have been taken.

281. Before 1980 product patents were protected only in those fields of use for which they were registered. Since the amendments in 1980 the principle of *absolute product protection* is applied. However, in some circumstances the protection might be limited solely to certain fields of use.[1] For example, where a protected invention is applied in a completely different field and this shows an inventive step which is not obvious to a person skilled in the art, then the use of the invention is not necessarily considered to be an infringement.[2]

1. Government Bill 1980/139 p. 3.
2. M. Koktvedgaard & M. Levin p. 245.

282. Where a process is protected by a process patent, third parties are prohibited from using the process or from offering such a process for use in Finland (Sect. 3, subpara. 2). Process patent is closely linked to indirect product protection. Indirect product protection prohibits the offering, putting on the market or use of a product obtained by a protected process, or the importing or possessing of such a product for these purposes (Sect. 3, subpara. 3). This provision strengthens protection for process patents and is important mainly for the chemical and pharmaceutical industries.

283. It may be difficult for the proprietor of a process patent to prove that a product is manufactured using the process. However, since 1996 Section 57a of the Patents Act contains a presumption rule in accordance with Article 34 of the TRIPS

Agreement. It provides that if there is a process patent for the manufacturing of a product, then any identical product shall be deemed to have been obtained by the patented process unless otherwise proven.[1]

1. Compare with Art. 75 of the CPC.

284. Contrary to other kinds of patent protection, indirect protection has *international applicability*. For example where a process is patented in Finland and a product is manufactured using the process in another country in which the process is not protected, then the product may not be imported to Finland. Thus, protection in Finland with regard to products manufactured using a protected process extends to all products manufactured using the same process, whether or not they are manufactured in Finland.[1]

1. M. Koktvedgaard & M. Levin p. 235.

285. Section 3, paragraph 2 prohibits *contributory infringement* of a patent. It provides that no party may, without the consent of the proprietor, supply or offer to supply any third parties not entitled to exploit an invention with the means of working the invention in Finland in relation to an essential element of the invention where such party knows, or it is evident from the circumstances, that the means are suitable and intended for working the invention. In other words, the means for working an invention may not be marketed or sold to anybody who is not allowed to work the invention.

286. *The scope of protection.* The scope of protection is to be determined by the claims, and the description may serve as guidance in interpreting the claims (Sect. 39). The claims specify what is protected and, therefore, anything not mentioned in the claims is not protected. They define the boundaries of protection, whereas the description and illustrations serve merely as aids in interpreting the patent. Even though Section 39 provides that the description may serve as guidance, this does not mean that other documents may not be used in the interpretation. For example, the correspondence between the applicant and the Patent Office or minutes from later proceedings may be used in some circumstances.

287. There has been an extensive discussion in the Nordic literature concerning *equivalence*. According to the theory of equivalence, the scope of protection extends to technically similar replacements or substitutes (equivalents). Thus, the claims would not be interpreted literally, but extensively. However, it has been argued that this theory is just another way of saying that a person skilled in the art regards two inventions as similar.[1]

1. M. Koktvedgaard & M. Levin pp. 245–246, B. Godenhielm (1990) pp. 93–115.

288. In addition to the above rules, there are some other rules that might help in determining the scope of protection. The scope of protection is to be determined by a person skilled in the art as an *overall assessment*. Regard must be had to the characteristics of the specific invention and to the field of technology in general. Normally, *changes of dimension* do not affect the protection.

289. Markings on goods and the obligation to provide information. It is not required for the enforceability of a patent that the patented goods are marked that a patent has been applied for or granted. Normally such markings are only made in order to promote sales of the product. Where such markings are used or the applicant or proprietor indicates in any other way that a patent has been applied for or granted, without at the same time indicating the number of the application or the patent, then he is required on request to furnish such a number without delay (Sect. 56, para. 2). However, the use of such a marking despite the fact that no patent has been applied for or granted in relation to the goods might be prohibited by Section 2 of the Unfair Trade Practices Act.

§7. Limitations and Exceptions to the Scope of Patent Protection – Compulsory Licences

290. Exhaustion. Until recently, patents in Finland were subject to national exhaustion. However, in 1993 the Patents Act was harmonised with the practice of the European Court of Justice and the principle of free movement of goods. Since that amendment the principle of regional (community) exhaustion has been applied.[1] This means that the exclusive right does not apply to the use of a patented product that has been put on the market within the EEA[2] by the proprietor or with his consent (Sect. 3, para. 3, subpara. 2).

1. Act No. 1409 of 18 December 1992.
2. The European Economic Area.

291. The exhaustion of rights is general, which means that it applies to all measures taken after putting the product on the market. The product may be freely sold, rented, imported, exported, etc. within the EEA. It may also be repaired, but major restoration with the character of production of new products probably falls within the scope of protection.

292. Regional (community) exhaustion accords with the principle of free movements of goods within the EEA. Thus, parallel importation is allowed within the EEA as long as the products have been put on the market with the consent of the proprietor. However, where the products have been put on the market outside of the EEA, or where they have been put on the market without the consent of the proprietor, the parallel importation of patented goods is prohibited. Where the products have been put on the market by someone other than the proprietor with rights based on a compulsory licence, then the products are not considered to have been put on the market with the consent of the proprietor.[1] However, if the proprietor puts the product on the market within the EEA in a country in which the product is not patentable, then the patent rights within the EEA are exhausted.[2] In a case where, for example, a licensee exceeds his rights under the agreement, the patent rights for the products manufactured under the licence are not exhausted.[3]

1. *See* the judgment of the ECJ in case 19/84 *Pharmon* v. *Hoechst* [1985] ECR 2281.
2. *See* the judgment of the ECJ in case 187/80 *Merck* v. *Stephar* [1981] ECR 2063.
3. M. Koktvedgaard & M. Levin p. 238.

293. Non-commercial use. Section 3, paragraph 3, subparagraph 1 provides that the exclusive right shall not apply to use which is not commercial. The words 'not commercial' shall be interpreted narrowly and they are used instead of expressions such as 'industrial and commercial activity' or 'business activity' in order to limit the scope of application of the exception. However, the exception does apply not only to private use of a patented invention, but also to other forms of non-commercial use.[1] A patent may be used for example in scientific research or university education for demonstration purposes. Nevertheless, the exception cannot be applied to protected equipment which is used in the educational process itself.[2]

   1. However, compare this with the following rather old Supreme Court decisions.
      Supreme Court judgment 1920 II 926
      X had manufactured protected devices to be used in his agricultural practice. The Supreme Court held this to be an infringement of the rights of the proprietor.
      Supreme Court judgment 1939 II 595
      The Supreme Court regarded the use of a patent by the national railway company to be commercial use.
   2. M. Jacobson & E. Tersmeden & L. Törnroth p. 112. Compare this with Art. 27(a) of the CPC.

294. Experiments and preparation of medicine. Protected inventions as such may be used in experiments (Sect. 3, para. 3, subpara. 3). Such use is also allowed in business activities for research purposes. As long as the use is for experimental purposes, 'reverse engineering' and other methods used in order to examine and analyse inventions made by others are allowed.[1]

   1. However, in C-316/95 *Generics* v. *Smith Kline* it was held that it constitutes an infringement to supply the national authority with a medicine for which another holds a patent in order to obtain an authorisation to put the medicine on the market.

295. The preparation in a pharmacy of a medicine prescribed by a physician in individual cases is also allowed, even though the medicine or the process is protected (Sect. 3, para. 3, subpara. 4). It should be noted that such preparation concerns individual cases and, thus, the medicine may not be manufactured in stock.

296. Right of prior use. Section 4 provides that in some circumstances a person who was exploiting the invention at the time when another filed a patent application for the said invention, may continue to exploit it regardless of the patent. This is an important exception to the rule that the first person to file the application acquires exclusive rights to the invention.

297. There are five requirements which must be fulfilled for somebody to obtain right of prior use. Firstly, the person must have exploited the invention or made substantial preparations for exploitation.[1] Any kind of exploitation is sufficient, i.e. everything that could constitute an infringement, such as importation. Substantial preparations may be either technical or commercial in character. They must be made expressly in order to prepare for the use of the invention, which, for example, does not include further examination of the patent.

   1. However, if the invention has become known to the public, it obviously lacks novelty and can no longer be patented.

298. Secondly, the exploitation must not constitute an evident abuse in relation to the applicant. Where somebody has, for example, obtained the necessary knowledge relating to the invention through industrial espionage, he cannot obtain right to prior use. However, as long as he acts in good faith, then he may obtain the right. Thirdly, the exploitation must be commercial. Any kind of commercial use satisfies the requirement. Right of prior use cannot be obtained where the use is non-commercial but, on the other hand, the user may continue to use the invention, since the exclusive rights extend only to commercial use.

Supreme Court judgment 1970 II 79
X had used the invention once before Y had filed an application concerning the same invention. The Supreme Court considered that X had used the invention commercially before the filing of the application and thus X acquired the right to prior use.

299. Fourthly, the invention must have been exploited in Finland. Finally, the invention must have been exploited at the time of filing the application.

300. The right of prior use is not an exclusive right, but exists only in relation to the proprietor. The person is entitled only to continue the exploitation of the invention and is protected from infringement claims from the proprietor. He cannot, however, bring an action against third parties or transfer the right to someone else, except when it is transferred together with the business in which it is exploited.

301. International traffic. Section 5 provides that foreign vessels, aircraft or other means of transport may be used in Finland when temporarily entering Finland irrespective of whether they contain patented inventions. In some circumstances spare parts and accessories for aircraft may also be imported and used in repairs notwithstanding the issuing of a patent. This provision is based on Article 5ter of the Paris Convention.

302. Compulsory licences. The provisions on compulsory licences have two main aims. Firstly, protection of domestic industry and other mainly political or social objectives. Secondly, the provisions prevent patent holders from misusing their legal monopolies in a way that is economically damaging for society. Historically, the first of these aims was the main objective of compulsory licencing, whereas the monopoly arguments have appeared later.[1]

1. M. Koktvedgaard (1965).

303. The compulsory licencing provisions in the Patents Act are found in Sections 45–50. The main forms of compulsory licencing are compulsory licencing for non-working patents (Sect. 45), for dependent patents (Sect. 46) and compulsory licencing in the public interest (Sect. 47).[1] Furthermore, Section 48 concerns compulsory licences where the invention was in commercial use at the time when the patent application was published.[2]

1. K. Pfanner p. 4.
2. Compare with the right of prior use.

304. Sections 49 and 50 provide some general principles for compulsory licencing. The Court may grant a compulsory licence only to a person deemed to be technically and economically in a position to exploit the invention in an acceptable manner and in accordance with the terms of the licence. Before filing a claim for a compulsory licence, the applicant must have made a verifiable effort to obtain a licence from the proprietor on reasonable commercial terms.[1] A compulsory licence gives no exclusive rights to the licensee, and thus the proprietor may exploit the invention and grant licences to other licensees. Moreover, a compulsory licence may be transferred only as part of the business in which it is exploited (Sect. 49). A compulsory licence is granted by a court of law, which also specifies the terms of the licence (Sect. 50).

1. This provision was amended in order to harmonise with Art. 31 of the TRIPS Agreement.

305. Section 45 concerns *non-working patents*. It provides that, where three years have elapsed from the date of issue of the patent and four years have elapsed from the application date and the invention has not been used in Finland to a reasonable extent, a third party may obtain a compulsory licence for the patent, if the proprietor, or a licensee, has no legitimate reasons for the non-working. The proprietor may work the invention himself or may grant licences and since 1996 importation has also been considered to meet the requirement for use of the patent.[1]

1. Government Bill 1995/161 p. 9.

306. Section 46 concerns *dependent patents*. It provides that the proprietor of a patent on an invention whose exploitation depends on a patent held by another person may obtain a compulsory licence to exploit the invention protected by such patent if it is deemed reasonable in view of the importance of the former invention or for other special reasons. It should be noted that only a person who has obtained a patent on the dependent invention may be granted a compulsory licence. Where he has only a licence for the dependent invention, Section 46 cannot be applied.

307. Section 47 concerns compulsory licences in *considerable public interest*. It provides that, where considerable public interest warrants, a compulsory licence may be granted to a person who wishes to exploit commercially an invention for which another person holds a patent. Public interest refers mainly to state security and matters concerning health and social security, but it also refers to political and economic reasons. Economic reasons might be e.g. the public interest in making technological progress available in a country and making the products covered by patents available in sufficient quantity and at an adequate price level.[1] However, Section 47 may be applied only in extraordinary circumstances where public interests of extreme importance are involved.[2] Furthermore, the provision cannot be applied where the same result can be achieved by applying other legislation, e.g. competition law.

1. K. Pfanner p. 9.
2. B. Godenhielm (1983) p. 414.

308. Finally, compulsory licences may be granted where a person has been exploiting an invention at the time when a patent application with regard to the same invention became public.[1] Section 48 provides that any person who, in Finland, was exploiting commercially an invention which is the subject of a patent application, at the time when the application documents became public, may be entitled to a compulsory licence. The provision requires that there be special reasons for granting such a licence and that the person did not have, or could not easily have obtained, knowledge of the application. The provision is also applicable where the person has made substantial preparations for the exploitation of the invention.

1. Section 48 recalls the right of prior use as provided in Sect. 4, but Sect. 48 is applicable in situations where the invention has been used after the filing of the application but before the documents have become public.

309. Even though the provisions concerning compulsory licences might be important in principle, they are seldom applied in practice. There has been only one case before the Finnish courts, and therefore it is difficult to say in what circumstances they might become applicable.[1] However, even though the provisions are very seldom applied, their mere existence might encourage the parties to agree about licences.

1. *Medipolar* v. *Imperial Chemical Industries (ICI)* Court of Appeal of Helsinki judgment of 31 December 1979. The case is published in: Jukka Kemppinen (ed.): Immateriaalioikeudellisia oikeustapauksia [Cases in Intellectual Property Law]; and commented on in: NIR No. 1 1985 pp. 91–98.

310. Expropriation. If Finland is at war or threatened by war, then the Government may decree that the right to a given invention shall be surrendered to the State or to another party designated by the Government (Sect. 75). Reasonable compensation is to be paid for the expropriated patent. The *Act on Inventions of Importance for Defence* contains further provisions on expropriation, secrecy and application for patents.[1]

1. Act on Inventions of Importance for Defence No. 551 of 15 December 1967.

§8. Duration of Protection – Maintenance and Termination of Patent Protection

311. The maximum term of protection. The maximum term of protection for a patent is 20 years. The term begins from the date of filing the application (Sect. 40). In order for the patent to be maintained, the prescribed fees are to be paid each year.

312. However, protection for medicines may be extended by a maximum of five years in accordance with Council Regulation (EEC) No. 1768/92 concerning *supplementary protection certificates for medicinal products*.[1] This is effective in Finland and Section 70a refers directly to the regulation, without reproducing the substantial rules of the regulation in the Patents Act. Sections 70b–70e of the Patents Act and Sections 52d–52p of the Patents Decree provide details of the application procedure, the maintenance of protection, the fees, etc.

1. Council Regulation (EEC) No. 1768/92 of 18 June 1992 concerning the creation of supplementary protection certificates for medicinal products.

313. The patent that obtains extended protection (the basic patent) may be a Finnish patent or an EPC-patent valid in Finland. In order to be able to obtain extended protection, the patented medicine must have authorisation to be put on the market as a medicine. Even though it is the product that obtains the certificate, the basic patent need not be a product patent, but may also be a process patent or a use patent. However, it is possible to obtain only one certificate per product. The certificate confers on the specific products the same rights as the basic patent. The application for a certificate is to be filed at the Finnish Patent Office.

314. Extended protection takes effect at the end of the term of the basic patent. The term of extended protection is a period equal to the period which elapsed between the date on which the application for the basic patent was filed and the date of the first authorisation to place the product on the market, minus a period of five years. However, the duration of the certificate may not exceed five years.

315. The European Parliament and Council Regulation (EC) No. 1610/96 concerning *supplementary protection certificates for plant protection products*[1] is also effective in Finland and contains rules corresponding to those of the regulation for medicines.

1. Council Regulation (EC) No. 1610/96 concerning the adoption of a supplementary protection certificate for plant protection products.

316. Maintaining the protection. In order to maintain the patent protection, fees must be paid annually for each year beginning after the issuing of the patent (Sect. 40, para. 2).[1] The fees for the first two years become payable when the fee for the third year is due. On request, the Patent Office may grant the applicant or a proprietor who is the inventor respite in respect of payment, where he experiences serious difficulty in paying the annual fees (Sect. 42).

1. Note that due to Sect. 8, para. 6 the applicant must also pay annual fees during the application procedure.

317. The annual fee is to be paid on the last day of the calendar month during which the fee year begins. If the proprietor does not pay the fee by the due date, then he must pay the annual fees, together with the prescribed additional fees, within six months of the said due date (Sect. 41, para. 3). Even where the proprietor has not paid the fee within the extended period of time, the patent may still be upheld if the proprietor shows that he has done everything that can reasonably be required of him (Sect. 71a).

Patent Office decision of 26 October 1995 (Jonaco GmbH)
The Belgian agent of the applicant had, contrary to the instructions, intentionally not paid the fifth annual fee by the due date, in order to prevent the applicant's debt to him from increasing. The Board of Appeal held that in applying Section 71a the applicant and the agent shall be comparable. Thus, the applicant can have no recourse to the fact that it is the agent, and not the applicant himself, who has failed to make payment by the due date. The applicant was therefore not considered to

have done everything that can be reasonably required of him to observe the time limit. The patent was terminated.

318. Section 71a applies to all cases (except loss of priority date) where the applicant or proprietor has suffered loss of rights because he has failed to take action at the Patent Office within the specified time limit, but he has done everything that reasonably can be required of him to observe the time limit. If he takes action in such a case within two months of the time when the non-compliance ceases, and in any event not later than one year after the expiration of the time limit, then the Patent Office is to declare that the act shall be deemed to have been performed within the prescribed time limit.

Patent Office decision 75/P/96 of 27 August 1996 (Dow Chemical Company)
The Board of Appeal held that Section 71a could be applied in a case where the applicant had not complied with the period of 30 months for an international application, as provided in Section 31, paragraph 2. The agent had asked the applicant twice whether he wished to continue with the application in Finland. The first letter was sent half a year prior to the expiry of the time limit. The second letter disappeared in the post. It was considered that the first letter was too early for the applicant to take action. He waited for the second letter, which did not arrive. Both the applicant and the agent were considered to have done everything that could be reasonably required of them to observe the time limit.

319. The time limits have been extended by virtue of Section 71a *inter alia* also in cases where the applicant, owing to illness, was incapable of taking care of his business, where there were problems with telex transmissions between the applicant and the agent, where the delay was due to a mistake made by a summer assistant and to human error, and where an agent had transferred a part of his business to another agent and all of the information pertaining to that had not been transferred so that some time limits had consequently not been observed.[1]

1. Patent Office decision 71/P/96 of 27 August 1996, Patent Office decision 14/P/96 of 27 August 1996, Patent Office decision 162/P/96 of 27 August 1996 and Patent Office decision 21/P/96 of 27 August 1996 (Board of Appeal judgments).

320. Termination. If the prescribed annual fee is not paid, then the patent will lapse as from the start of the fee year for which the fee has not been paid (Sect. 51). Thus, the proprietor does not need to withdraw in order to get the patent terminated, but the patent will be terminated automatically when he fails to pay the fee. However, the patent may be upheld if the proprietor pays the fees and additional fees within an extended time limit as provided in Section 41, paragraph 3 and Section 71a. The patent may also be terminated formally, e.g. in order to avoid court proceedings, if the proprietor surrenders the patent in writing to the Patent Office (Sect. 54).

321. Revocation of a patent. A patent may be declared invalid by the court only on the grounds provided in Section 52, which is harmonised with Article 138 of the EPC. Firstly, the patent may be declared invalid if it does not satisfy the requirements for patentability as provided in Sections 1 and 2, including the requirement of novelty. Secondly, it may be declared invalid where the description is not clear enough to enable a person skilled in the art to perform the invention. Thirdly, it may be declared invalid if it contains subject matter that was not included in the application as filed. Finally, it may be declared invalid where the applicant has extended the scope of protection after the Patent Office has given notice, as provided in Section 19, that the application can be accepted.

322. It should be noted that a patent cannot be declared invalid on grounds other than those referred to above. Therefore, a patent cannot be declared invalid where, for example, the claims are unclear, where the Patent Office has granted a patent based on an application containing two independent inventions, where a patent has been granted even though the application does not fulfil the requirements for application as provided in Section 8, except for the description, or where there has been a procedural failure.[1]

1. M. Jacobson & E. Tersmeden & L. Törnroth p. 317.

323. It has been established in court practice that a patent may be declared *partially invalid*, even though the Patents Act does not provide for such a possibility. Where, for example, the patent includes many inventions and the proprietor is not entitled to all of them, or where some of the claims do not satisfy the necessary requirements, the court may declare the patent invalid in respect of those parts of the patent. In practice the court declares a patent partially invalid by changing the wording of and restricting the claims.[1]

1. E.g. in Supreme Court judgment 1984 II 117. P.-L. Haarmann p. 122.

324. Where the court has declared a patent invalid in accordance with Section 52, the patent is to be regarded as invalid *ex tunc* or *ab initio*. This means that the patent is to be regarded as not having existed at all. By virtue of Section 61 no penalty or compensation may be ordered against a potential infringer where the patent has been revoked or declared invalid. However, the effect of invalidity on a contractual relationship depends on the actual contract. In respect of licence payments, the patent is regarded as invalid *ex nunc*, which means that licence payments already paid cannot be reclaimed.[1] The invalidity of a patent is general, i.e. it is invalid in relation to any person, not only to the parties to the proceedings.

1. M. Koktvedgaard & M. Levin p. 260.

325. The District Court of Helsinki is the sole *competent court* of first instance in respect of patent cases in Finland (Sect. 65). The Court is, in addition to its normal composition, assisted by two technical experts, who give their views on the matters considered. The technical assistants are appointed by the Court (Sect. 66). The proceedings may be instituted, with the exception referred to above, by any person who suffers prejudice on account of the patent or by the public prosecutor (Sect. 52, para. 3). The proceedings are brought against the proprietor, not against the Patent Office, but the Patent Office and licensees are to be informed of the proceedings (Sect. 64).

Patents, Ch. 2

326. *EPC patents* effective in Finland are declared invalid in Finland on the same grounds as Finnish patents. Even though Section 52 has been harmonised with the EPC and the courts are presented with the same material, there are no guarantees that EPC patents will be treated equally in the courts of the various EPC countries.[1]

1. M. Koktvedgaard & M. Levin p. 261.

§9. Infringement and Remedies

327. Sections 57 to 68 provide for various kinds of remedies and sanctions in cases of infringement of a patent, the nature of which depends on the culpability of the offending party.[1] Firstly, the court may *forbid any person who infringes the exclusive right from continuing or repeating the act* (Sect. 57, para. 1).[2] The court may also order that patented products manufactured without the consent of the proprietor, or objects whose use would constitute an infringement, shall be *altered, impounded, destroyed or surrendered* to the injured party against payment (Sect. 59, para. 1). However, this provision does not apply to anyone who has acquired the objects in good faith and who has not himself infringed the patent. Furthermore, Section 59, paragraph 2 provides that the objects may be *seized* if it is reasonable to assume that the infringer has committed an offence against an intellectual property right as provided under Chapter 48, Section 2 of the Penal Code.

1. The Act does not require any notice letter to the defendant prior to initiating infringement proceedings. However, such notice is required by the ethical rules of the Finnish Bar Association (R. Hilli *et al.* (1996) p. 179).
2. Please *see* §6 for the scope of exclusive rights and what constitutes infringement of them.

328. Section 68 provides that the Court may grant an *interlocutory injunction* during the proceedings on use of the patent or *seize* patented products manufactured without the consent of the proprietor. The plaintiff may be required to provide security for any damage or inconvenience the respondent may suffer due to the action. The Court may also grant interlocutory injunctions based on the general provisions concerning interim measures in Chapter 7 of the Procedural Code. In practice, the courts are restrictive in granting interlocutory injunctions.

329. Where a person intentionally infringes a patent, he may be punished either under Section 57, paragraph 2 of the Patents Act or Chapter 48, Section 2 of the Penal Code. Where the infringement is liable to cause considerable damage to the injured party, the infringer may be sentenced to imprisonment or fined for an *industrial property offence*. Otherwise he is liable to a fine for a *violation of a patent right*. Indictment for a violation of a patent right may be brought by the Public Prosecutor only at the request of the injured party.

330. The most important remedies, however, are compensation and damages. Firstly, the infringer must always pay *reasonable compensation for the exploitation* of the invention. Secondly, he must pay *damages* where the infringement has caused injury to the other party (Sect. 58, para. 1). The *compensation* is equal to the amount that normally would have been paid in licence fees for such exploitation under an agreement. The infringer must pay compensation even where the proprietor has suffered no damages whatsoever. Thus, the compensation is a minimum indemnity to which the injured party is always entitled.

331. Where the injured party has suffered other injuries, he is also entitled to *damages*. In order to secure full damages he must show that the injuries exceed those due to loss of potential licence fees (the compensation). Normally the infringer has to pay damages for lost profits. However, damages for declining sales, market damages and direct losses and costs may also become payable. It should be noted that it is the injuries of the proprietor that determine the damages, not the profits of the infringer. The infringer is not obliged to transfer his profits to the proprietor, but on the other hand, the compensation and damages are not limited to his profits.[1]

1. P.-L. Haarmann p. 118.

332. The amount and type of damages and compensation depends on the *degree of culpability* of the infringer. Where the infringer has acted intentionally or negligently, he must pay reasonable compensation and full damages. In the case of slight negligence, the compensation and damages may be adjusted accordingly. Where the infringer has acted neither intentionally nor negligently, he is liable to pay compensation only if, and to the extent, that this is considered reasonable (Sect. 58, para. 2).

333. In considering culpability, the knowledge of the infringer that he was infringing a patent is not relevant, but it is what he should have known that is relevant. In principle everybody is deemed to have knowledge of all patents and published applications. However, in practice only importers and manufacturers have a strict duty to make investigations concerning patents and applications. Others, such as distributors, wholesalers, etc., do not have such a strict duty to make inquiries.[1]

1. P.-L. Haarmann p. 119.

334. Compensation and damages may be obtained only for infringements suffered within *five years* before instituting proceedings (Sect. 58, para. 3). However, the five years rule is not applied where the proceedings are instituted within one year of the period of lodging an opposition or, if an opposition has been lodged, within one year of the date of the decision to maintain the patent (Sect. 60, para. 2).

335. There is no liability for remedies or punishment under the Patents Act for exploiting the invention of another person, which is subject to a patent application, prior to the time at which the application documents became public.[1] After the documents have become public, but before the issuing of the patent, there is no liability to punishment and damages shall be paid only if, and to the extent, that they are held to be reasonable, provided that the application results in a patent (Sect. 60).[2] During this period, an infringer may, however, be liable to pay compensation.[3] All of the remedies are available only from the time of issuing of the patent. Until the patent has been granted, protection extends only to the subject matter disclosed *both* in the claims of the application *and* the claims of the patent issued.

1. In some circumstances Sect. 4 of the Unfair Trade Practices Act or contractual arrangements may also provide sanctions prior to the publishing of the application.
2. M. Jacobson & E. Tersmeden & L. Törnroth p. 317.
3. The documents are made available to the public as from the date of issue of the patent. Nevertheless, they shall be made available to the public 18 months after the filing date or the priority date, regardless of whether the patent has been issued (Sect. 22).

336. Where a *patent has been revoked* by a final decision or *declared invalid* in a final court decision, no penalty, payment of compensation or other measures may be ordered. Finally, not only the proprietor, but also a licensee, regardless of whether the licence is exclusive, is entitled to institute proceedings in the court because of an infringement.[1]

1. P.-L. Aro (1985) p. 366.

337. In the event of uncertainty, proceedings for a *declaratory judgment* may be instituted in order to establish whether an invention or a commercial activity is protected by a patent. Such proceedings may be instituted by the proprietor, a licensee or any person who intends to carry on such activity (Sect. 63).

§10. Overlapping and Relation to Other Intellectual Property Laws

338. Converting a patent application into a utility model application. Section 8 of the Utility Model Act[1] provides that a patent application may be converted into a utility model application. Where the patent application is filed after 1 January 1996, it is to remain pending regardless of such conversion.[2] The utility model application is to be deemed to have been filed on the same date as the patent application was filed. The provisions concerning conversion correspond to those of the German and Danish utility model acts.[3]

1. Utility Model Act No. 800 of 10 May 1991 (as amended).
2. However, if it has been filed before that date it is to be deemed to have been withdrawn.
3. K. Roitto pp. 170–172.

339. Plants may obtain protection based on the *Act on Breeder's Rights*[1] in accordance with the UPOV-conventions of 1961 and 1978.[2] The Act on Breeder's Rights will be discussed below in Chapter 7 concerning plant variety protection. In some circumstances the protection provided by the Patents Act and the Act on Breeder's Rights for a plant variety or for a process for the production for a plant variety might in practice overlap.[3]

1. Act on Breeder's Rights No. 789 of 21 August 1992.
2. The UPOV-convention was amended in 1991.
3. However, note that Art. 92 of the EC Council Regulation on Plant Variety Rights (EC Council Regulation 2100/94 [1994] L227/1) provides that the holder of a Community Plant Variety Right (CPVR) is not permitted to enforce national patent or plant variety rights for the same variety. Once a CPVR has been granted the national rights to the same variety become ineffective.

340. The Unfair Trade Practices Act. Section 1 of the Unfair Trade Practices Act is a general clause prohibiting any practice that is against fair trade practice or otherwise unfair towards another trader. This provision might also be applicable in some circumstances to an infringement of a patent, e.g. before the patent has been granted.

341. Section 4 concerns *trade secrets and confidentiality.* It provides that no one may without justification obtain, or attempt to obtain, information regarding a trade secret, or use or disclose information thus obtained. Where somebody has obtained a trade secret from another knowing that the other has obtained the information without justification, he may not use or disclose such information. This provision might be applicable, for example, to trade secrets concerning inventions for which patents have not yet been sought. It might also be applied in relation to know-how in patent licences.

Chapter 3. Utility Models

§1. Sources – Legislation

Bibliography:
Feiring, K., 'Finska nyttighetsmodellagen – kunde den ha gjorts bättre?' [The Finnish Utility Model Act – Could It Have Been Done Better?], NIR 1992, pp. 200–204;
Haarmann, P.-L., *'Immateriaalioikeuden oppikirja'* [A Textbook of Intellectual Property Rights], Helsinki 1994;
Hiltunen, P., 'Bruksmönsterskydd' [The Protection of Utility Models], NIR 1986, pp. 457–461;
Kolster, A., 'Bruksmönster i Finland' [Utility Models in Finland], NIR 1987, pp. 287–294.

Official documents and publications:
Hyödyllisyysmallitoimikunnan mietintö [Report of the Utility Models Committee] 1986:48.

342. The Finnish Utility Model Act (No. 800 of 1991) and Utility Model Decree (No. 1419 of 1991) entered into force on 1 January 1992. The Act was modelled on the (West) German Utility Model Act. Over the last four years, however, the Act has been revised with respect to the needs of inventors, without making the registration procedure too complicated.[1]

1. Government Bill No. 232 of 1990 – as amended by Government Bill No. 25 of 1992, No. 215 of 1992 and No. 47 of 1995. *See also* K. Feiring p. 200.

343. Utility model law is internationally regulated by the Convention of the Union of Paris for the Protection of Industrial Property (1883) (Treaty Series 36/70 and 43/75). Article 1 of the Paris Convention concerns utility model rights. The Paris Convention does not commit the signatories to using utility model law to protect inventions. However, the Paris Convention does contain central provisions on national treatment, minimum protection and priority, which also apply in utility model law.

§2. The Protection of Utility Models

344. The Finnish Utility Model Act of 1991 protects minor technical inventions which do not achieve the level of inventive step required for patent rights. The application procedure for utility model rights is simpler, faster and more advantageous than the corresponding procedure for patents.[1] By protecting small inventions, utility model law also prevents erosion in the value of the patent system.[2]

1. P. Hiltunen pp. 458–459.
2. A. Kolster p. 288.

345. In 1996 the Patent Office received 638 applications for utility model rights, of which 452 were registered. In only a small number of cases (20) were the applicants foreign. Utility model rights protect technical inventions which can be commercially exploited (Sect. 1.2). The explicit requirement whereby a technical solution had to embody a shape or construction or combination thereof of a device was discontinued in 1996.[1] The matter usually concerns a small, simple, technical solution, which is why utility model rights are sometimes referred to as a *minor patent*. Inventions protected by model utility rights partly comprise technical ideas and solutions which are not patentable but which are not obvious to an expert and partly small inventions and improvements which in principle are patentable but which will be used only for a short time or which are of such minor commercial value that utility model rights provide an adequate degree of protection. Such protection does not cover processes, nor does it apply to plant and animal species. Processes are protected by patents. The invention is subject to the same claims of evidence of originality as are patents, i.e. the invention must be new in relation to what was known before the day of application and must differ clearly[2] from what was known earlier (inventive step).[3]

1. Government Bill No. 47 of 1995.
2. Compare to Sect. 2 of the Finnish Patents Act, 'differ essentially from'.
3. P.-L. Haarmann pp. 128–129.

346. The creator of the invention, or the person to whom the rights of the creator have been transferred, may apply to the Patent Office for registration of a model utility right. The granting of a model utility right gives the holder the exclusive right to commercial exploitation of the protected invention (Sect. 1). According to Section 3, an exclusive right means that without the consent of the holder no one may exploit an invention by making, selling or using a protected product. An exclusive right also provides protection against the actions of a third party not authorised to exploit the invention, who plans to offer or supply a means for its use, which constitutes some essential part thereof, provided that the said third party knew or ought to have known that this means was suited for the said use. The exclusive right does not restrict non-commercial use.[1]

1. The Act was amended in 1995 to include a provision on indirect utility infringement, Government Bill No. 47 of 1995.

347. Applications go through a so-called application procedure. During the application procedure (Sect. 12) the Registering Authority only examines whether the application satisfies the formal requirements of Section 1.2 and whether exploitation of the invention would be contrary to public morals or public order. Evidence of originality and inventive step are not examined unless the applicant expressly requests such examination.[1] The application must contain a description and one or more illustrations of the invention together with precise specifications of which utility right protection is sought.

1. K. Feiring p. 203.

348. The application procedure gives the applicant and third parties the right of appeal. Because the inventive step is not examined before registration, it is possible to register an invention which does not satisfy the legal requirements. For this reason the Finnish Utility Model Act contains provisions for declaring a registration null and void (Sects. 19–21). The greatest disadvantage with a utility model right is therefore the risk that it will be declared null and void. Any person may at any time submit such a claim to the Patent Office. The claimant must state the facts in support of the claim and pay a fee before the claim will be considered. The applicant may seek an advance assessment of the viability of the protection by requesting that, in return for a fee, the Patent Office makes an inquiry into the originality.

349. Under Section 8 of the Finnish Utility Model Act, a pending application for a patent may be converted into an application for a utility model right. The conversion must be made within ten years of the day on which the patent application was filed. Pending patent applications also remain pending after the application has been changed, which secures the rights of protection of the holder in situations where there is an infringement of solutions which were not included in the application for a utility model right.[1]

1. The change was made in 1995, Government Bill No. 47 of 1995.

350. A utility model right is first registered for a period of four years, following which it may be renewed for a further four years and thereafter for no longer than two additional years. The maximum period of protection is therefore ten years from the date on which the original application was filed (Sect. 25).

351. A utility model right may be assigned and licenced (Sects. 27–29) in accordance with the applicable principles of property law. Where an invention is not exploited, compulsory licencing (Sect. 30) may also be possible under certain conditions.

352. The measures available against infringements of a utility model right are equivalent to the system of sanctions available under patent law (Sects. 36–45): in the first instance this means issuing an injunction and awarding reasonable compensation, while in the case of serious offences, fines and imprisonment are possible. The District Court of Helsinki has sole competence in the first instance in cases involving utility model rights.

Chapter 4. Trademarks

§1. Sources – Legislation

Bibliography in Finnish or Nordic languages:
Drockila, L., *'Tavaramerkkien sekoitettavuudesta ja harhaanjohtavuudesta'* [The Confusing Similarity and Misleading Character of Trademarks], Lakimiesliiton kustannus, Helsinki 1986;
Haarmann, P.-L., *'Immateriaalioikeuden oppikirja'* [A Textbook of Intellectual Property Rights] 2nd ed., Lakimiesliiton kustannus, Helsinki 1994;
Hakulinen, Y.J., *'Tavaramerkkioikeus'* [The Law of Trademarks], WSOY, Helsinki 1954;
Karlsson, E., *'Skadestånd vid intrång i industriella rättigheter'* [Infringement of Industrial Property Rights and Damages], NIR No. 3, 1990, pp. 369–396;
Koktvedgaard, M. & Levin, M., *'Lärobok i immaterialrätt'* [A Textbook of Intellectual Property Rights], Norstedts Juridik, Stockholm 1995;
Kolve, P., *'Tavaramerkin käyttöpakko'* [On the Obligation to Use a Trademark] in Tavaramerkki [Trademarks], Lakimiesliiton kustannus, Helsinki 1983;
Lahtinen, S.-L., *'Tillämpningen av undantag för utstyrselskydd enligt art. 3.1.e direktiv 89/104/EEG (Finland)'* [On the Interpretation of Article 3.1.e of Directive 89/104/EEC (Finland)], NIR No. 4, 1996, pp. 547–548;
Lassen, B.S., *'Oversikt over norsk varemerkerett'* [A Review of Norwegian Trademark Law] 2 ed., Universitetesforlaget, Oslo 1997;
Levin, M., *'Noveller i varumärkesrätt'* [Developments in Trade Mark Law], Juristförlaget, Stockholm 1990;
Pehrson, L., *'Varumärken från konsumentsynpunkt'* [Trade Marks from the Consumer's Point of View], Liber förlag, Stockholm 1981;
Siponen, A., *'Tavaramerkin sekoitettavuus'* [The Confusing Similarity of Trademarks], in Tavaramerkki [Trademarks], Lakimiesliiton kustannus, Helsinki 1983;
Starell, J., *'Användningstvångets framtida utformning'* [The Future Form of Compulsory Use], NIR No. 1, 1992, pp. 34–55;
Tiili, V., *'Tavaramerkkien sekoitettavuus'* [The Confusing Similarity of Trademarks], LM No. 6, 1987, pp. 698–704;
Tiili, V. & Aro, P.-L., *'Yrityksen tavaramerkki- ja mallisuojaopas'* [An Enterprise's Guide to Trademarks and Registration of Designs] 1st ed., Kauppalehti Business Books, Jyväskylä 1986.

Bibliography in English:
Castrén, M. & Kolster, B., 'Non-confusing Use of Another's Trademark', in AIPPI Q 95 No. 7, 1988, pp. 134–146;
Hilli, R., *'Trade marks'*, Ch. 6.3 in Metaxas-Maranghidis, Intellectual Property Laws of Europe (Chansery Law Publishing, Chichester 1995), pp. 134–137;
Hilli, R. et al., 'Enforcement of Intellectual Property Rights – Procedure and Sanctions', in AIPPI Q 134A No. 4, 1996, pp. 175–180;

Kolster, B. et al., 'Trademarks: Conflicts with Prior Rights', in AIPPI Q 104 No. 4, 1991, pp. 65–68;
Nordman, E. et al., 'Enforcement of Intellectual Property Rights – Procedure and Sanctions', in AIPPI Q 134B No. 5, 1996, pp. 155–174;
Rissanen, K., 'Protection of Collective and Certification Marks', in AIPPI Q 72 No. 1, 1982, pp. 38–41;
Tommila, M. et al., 'Trademark Licensing and Franchising', in AIPPI Q116 No. 4, 1993, pp. 93–98;
Tommila, M. et al., 'House Marks', in AIPPI Q 107 No. 7, 1991, pp. 46–56.

Official documents and publications:
Government Bill 1962/128;
Government Bill 1983/37;
Government Bill 1992/302;
Government Bill 1995/135;
Kauppa- ja teollisuusministeriö KTM [Report of the Ministry of Trade and Industry] 39/1996, *'Tunnusmerkkilainsäädännön uudistamistarpeet'* [The Need to Revise Legislation on Marks];
SOU 1958:10, *'Förslag till varumärkeslag'*.

353. Historically, Nordic trademark law has been influenced by German law. The first Trademarks Act in Finland came into force in 1889 and was comprehensively revised in 1953.

354. Finland ratified the Paris Convention in 1921, since which time Finnish trademark law has been harmonised with it.

355. The current Finnish Trademarks Act (No. 7 of 10 January 1964) came into force on 1 June 1964 as a result of co-Nordic preparation.[1] Thereafter the Act has been amended several times.[2] By Act No. 30 of 25 January 1993 the Trademarks Act was amended in order to harmonise Finnish substantive trademark legislation with the Trademarks Directive.[3] Most recently the Trademarks Act was amended by Act No. 1715 of 22 December 1995 in order to meet the requirements for international registration as stipulated in the Madrid Protocol,[4] which has been in force in Finland since 1 April 1996. This amendment introduced important changes in the exhaustion, registration, renewal and duration of trademarks and in trademark application procedures.[5] Furthermore, the Community Trademark, as stipulated in the Community Trademark Regulation,[6] has been in force in Finland since 1 April 1996.

1. The Nordic trademark acts were originally constructed in a similar manner and the same principles applied to them. As time has passed, they have not always been amended in the same way. Also in court practice some rules have been applied differently and, therefore, there are now some differences in them. However, in most respects they are still quite similar.
    It might be noted that co-operation between the Nordic countries in the preparation work was conducted on a voluntary basis with no obligations for the countries either to be part of the co-operation or to comply with its outcome. Despite this, the trademark acts became harmonised in most respects.
2. The Trademarks Act has been amended by Acts No. 552 of 21 August 1970, No. 176 of 20 February 1976, No. 996 of 16 December 1983, No. 581 of 26 June 1992, No. 1038 of

13 November 1992, No. 13 of 25 January 1993 and No. 716 of 21 April 1995, Acts No. 1699 of 22 December 1995 and No. 1715 of 22 December 1995.
3. First Council Directive 89/104 of 21 December 1988.
4. Protocol Relating to the Madrid Agreement Concerning the International Registration of Marks (27 June 1989).
5. Decree No. 88 of 12 February 1996.
6. Council Regulation 40/94 of 20 December 1993 on the Community Trade Mark.

356. In addition to the Trademarks Act and Trademarks Decree, important sources of law are the judgments of the Supreme Court (SC), the Supreme Administrative Court (SAC) and the Court of Appeal of Helsinki. In several areas, however, there is rather little case law. Decisions on registration issued by the Board of Appeal of the National Board of Patents and Registration are therefore also important.

357. The Trademarks Act provides protection for all kinds of goods and services trademarks. The Collective Marks Act[1] provides protection for collective marks, i.e. collective trademarks used by commercial or industrial groups and associations. The Collective Marks Act also regulates the use of control marks on goods and services which are subject to control or supervision by a public authority, association or institution the duty of which is to control or supervise such goods and services.[2]

1. Collective Marks Act No. 795 of 5 December 1980, as amended by Act No. 40 of 25 January 1993.
2. R. Hilli, 'Trade Marks', Ch. 6.3 in Metaxas-Maranghidis, *Intellectual Property Laws of Europe*, p. 135.

§2. SUBJECT MATTER OF PROTECTION

I. Signs which may Serve as Trademarks

358. A trademark is a special symbol used to distinguish goods to be offered for sale or otherwise purveyed in business from similar goods offered or purveyed by others. The sole right to a trademark is acquired either by registration or by right of establishment (Sect. 1, para. 1). The provisions concerning goods are *mutatis mutandis* applicable to services (Sect. 1, para. 3). Service marks are used by hotels, travel agencies, insurance companies, banks, etc. in order to distinguish their services from those of others.

359. By virtue of Section 1, paragraph 2, any kind of trademark that can be represented graphically may be registered, i.e. such a mark must be visual and capable of being reproduced on paper,[1] and it must be possible, through the use of such a mark, to distinguish goods marketed in business from those of others. In particular, a trademark may consist of words, including personal names, figures, letters, numerals or the shape of goods or of their packaging. Slogans and sounds [sound marks] can also be represented graphically and may be registered.[2] Marks that cannot be represented graphically, e.g. odours, may not be registered. However, the requirement of graphical representability might be satisfied simply because the mark includes some visual elements.

1. M. Koktvedgaard & M. Levin p. 309.
2. The 'Ice cream van' melody of Ingman Foods was registered on 21 January 1995. The trademark consisted of a sound and was described by using notes. A tape recording of the melody was also included in the application.

360. Section 2, paragraph 2 provides that the sole right of use of symbols other than those business symbols defined in Section 1, paragraph 2 may be acquired by right of establishment. This means that trademarks which cannot be represented graphically, e.g. odours, may acquire protection as a trademark when they have become established.

II. Various Categories of Marks

361. Word marks consist of one or several words that form the name of the goods. The words may either be invented words or already existing words used in a semantically different manner. Marks that refer to or describe some quality of the goods are often preferred, but these may be difficult to register because of their lack of distinctiveness (Sect. 13, para. 1). A trademark lacking distinctiveness may, however, become protected by establishment. Invented words usually meet the requirement of distinctiveness more easily. A word mark must be pronounceable.

362. Letter and numerical marks consist of letters or numerals not forming a pronounceable word, e.g. AEG, IBM, 4711. Letter and numeral marks became registrable in Finland when Section 13 was harmonised with the Trademarks Directive (89/104).[1] Their distinctiveness is assessed on general principles.

1. Before 1993 the now repealed Sect. 13, para. 2 provided that letter and numeral marks may not be registered. However, they might have been registered in any case based on the *telle quelle*-rule or, in some cases, as figure marks. They could also be registered if they had acquired protection through establishment.

363. Figure marks may consist of geometrical figures, stylised letters, signs, symbols, animals, plants, mythological figures, drawings, pictures, natural products, etc., and of combinations of these. Three-dimensional marks, provided that they can be reproduced on paper, and marks that cover the goods or packaging may also be registered. Pictures or drawings of the concerned goods or services are easily considered to be descriptive.

364. Combined marks may consist of figures, words, letters or numerals. Where the word is written using a certain typeface and is decorated or stylised (a typical logo), then the subject of protection is the combined mark and not its elements.[1]

1. P.-L. Haarmann p. 154.

365. The *get-up, design, form or shape of the goods or of their packaging* may be protected by registration or by establishment as a mark.[1] The requirement of distinctiveness is especially strict and in some cases the mark may be registered only after it has become established. The package is used as a trademark especially in the food and cosmetics industry where it has become increasingly important. The 'Toblerone' chocolate bar is an example of protected packaging and goods, and striped toothpaste is an example of a protected form of goods. It has been argued that the requirements for packaging to acquire protection in Nordic law are less strict than those applicable to the goods themselves.[2] It should be noted that Article 3(1)(e) of the Trademark Directive[3] does not seem to be properly implemented in Section 5 of the Finnish Trademarks Act.[4]

1. In some countries protection may be obtained only through registration, e.g. in Germany, while in some other countries protection may not be obtained at all, e.g. England and Switzerland.
2. L. Pehrson p. 186.
3. First Council Directive 89/104 of 21 December 1988.
4. Section 5 provides that: 'The sole right to a trade symbol shall not apply to any part of the symbol which is intended mainly to render the goods or their packaging more suitable for their purpose, or else serves some purpose other than that of a trade symbol.' The wording of Sect. 5 and Art. 3(1)(c) differs considerably. Section 5 says nothing about the shape giving 'substantial value to the goods'. The Finnish Act should be applied in accordance with the Directive. It is not clear how Sect. 5 will be applied on this point. Whereas Art. 3(1)(e) concerns only the shape of the goods and registration, Sect. 5 also concerns the packaging of the goods and protection through right of establishment. In the other Nordic countries the Directive is implemented properly on this point. See e.g. S.-L. Lahtinen NIR No. 4, 1996.

366. The surnames of individuals, their addresses or trade names may always be used as a trade symbol in business unless its use is liable to cause confusion with the protected trademark of another, or with a name, an address or a trade name that another is already using lawfully in his business (Sect. 3, para. 1). The name or trade name of another may not be included in a trademark except where the trademark is the name of the applicant or where the trademark lacks distinguishing power or the branch of trade or kinds of goods concerned are different (Sect. 3, para. 3). Section 14, subparagraph 4 prohibits the registration of a trademark which is likely to give the impression of being a protected trade name, subsidiary company name, etc. of another.[1]

1. P.-L. Haarmann p. 161.

367. It should be noted that the use of a trademark in contravention of Section 3, paragraph 3 is always prohibited regardless of whether or not the said name is registered.

368. The *Act on Collective Marks*[1] regulates *association marks* and *control marks*. Section 1, paragraph 1 provides that a body corporate may, by means of registration in the same way as is stipulated in the Trademarks Act, or through establishment, acquire the exclusive right to an association mark. An association mark is one used by the members of the body in their professional activities. By right of establishment, the sole right to an association mark may also be acquired in respect of symbols other than those referred to above, i.e. symbols that cannot be represented graphically. Section 1, paragraph 2 provides that a public authority, association or institution the duty of which is to check or supervise goods or services or to issue statements regarding them may, by means of registration, acquire the exclusive right to a special mark for use on goods or services subject to the said control

Trademarks, Ch. 4

or supervision (a control mark). Association marks and control marks are called collective marks. Except where otherwise provided, the Trademarks Act applies *mutatis mutandis* to collective marks.

1. The Act on Collective Marks No. 795 of 5 December 1980 as amended by Act No. 40 of 21 January 1993.

369. Corporate signs.[1] A corporate sign is a symbol used to identify a company, a group or some other particular organisation. As opposed to identifying specific goods or services supplied by the organisation, the corporate sign is a symbol for all of its goods and services. Moreover, a corporate sign is used to symbolise the organisation itself and all of its activities and operations and to reinforce its goodwill. These signs are, therefore, by their very nature more closely related to trade names than to trademarks. Corporate signs have become increasingly important for the goodwill and public image of companies, which invest large sums of money in creating corporate images and corporate signs to stand for them.[2]

1. Also called corporate identifiers or house marks.
2. M. Tommila *et al.* Q 107 p. 46.

370. Corporate signs are usually dominants of trade names, trade names in specific typographical form, figures, pictures, other graphical symbols or some combination of these, which are understood to be symbols of the business operations concerned. They may also be melodies, combinations of colours, etc. A single economic entity may have different signs for various lines of business or operations.

371. Corporate signs are not regulated or protected as such in Finnish legislation. Protection may be acquired through the Trademarks Act, the Collective Marks Act or the Trade Names Act if the corporate sign is also a trademark or trade name. None of these Acts, however, provides proper and general protection. A graphical sign cannot be protected as a trade name. Under the Trade Names Act a graphical secondary symbol may enjoy protection but it cannot be registered and thus may be protected only by right of establishment. Protection by right of establishment does not meet the needs of enterprises, as it is often slow and fails to provide adequate legal security.[1]

1. KTM 39/1996 p. 34.

372. In practice the most common way to protect corporate signs is by registering the symbol as a trademark in all or almost all classes of goods and services. This, however, is inconvenient and expensive. As explained below in §8, the registration of a trademark may, on request of anyone who suffers inconvenience as a result of the said registration, be cancelled if the mark has not been used for the preceding five years and the proprietor cannot provide an acceptable reason for this. The case law concerning what is considered as an acceptable reason is strict. Thus the sign may be used by another as a trademark for any class of goods for which the first proprietor has not used the sign over the preceding five years (Sect. 26 of the Trademarks Act).

373. Corporate signs may also be protected in certain circumstances by the Unfair Trade Practices Act. Section 2 of the Act prohibits the use of untrue or misleading statements concerning one's own trade or that of another which are likely to influence the demand or supply of a commodity or to cause prejudice to the trade of another. Thus signs may not be used in a misleading way. The protection provided by the Act is insecure and does not suffice for proper protection. The Market Court can issue an injunction against using a sign or symbol in a misleading way but it cannot award damages. Such damages must be claimed in separate proceedings.

§3. Conditions of Protection

374. Protection of a trademark may be acquired either through registration or establishment (Sect. 1, para. 1 and Sect. 2, para. 1). Even though both registered and established trademarks are protected by the same rules, in practice it is easier to defend a registered trademark in legal proceedings. A trademark may also be protected by establishment and by registration at the same time. In such cases the fact of establishment may reinforce the protection, especially where the distinctiveness of the registered trademark as such is weak.[1]

1. SOU 1958:10 p. 219.

375. There are three requirements for a trademark to be eligible for registration:

1. the trademark can be represented graphically and is used in business,
2. the trademark is distinctive in the manner stipulated in Section 13, and
3. there are no impediments to registration of the kind referred to in Section 14.

376. The first condition has already been discussed in §2 above.

377. Section 13 provides that for a trademark to be eligible for registration it must be likely to *distinguish the goods of its proprietor* from those of others. Furthermore,

> '[a] mark that, either solely or with only a few alterations or additions, indicates the kind, quality, quantity, use, price, or place or time of manufacture of the goods shall not, as such, be regarded as distinctive. In assessing whether a trademark possesses distinguishing power, all factual circumstances shall be considered, particularly the length of time and extent to which the trademark has been used.' (Sect. 13)

378. There are two main reasons for the requirement of distinctiveness. Firstly, figures or reproductions of the goods which are too simple, or merely descriptive or generic words cannot, as such, achieve the very purpose of the mark, which is to distinguish the goods or services of one trader from those of another. Such a mark will not be regarded by the customers as individualising the product. Secondly, it would not be fair to allow such a mark to be reserved for one trader alone. The

Trademarks, Ch. 4

rights and opportunities of others to describe their products would, in such a case be limited, which would make the marketing of their products more difficult. These two motives should serve as guidelines when examining an application for registration.

379. A *descriptive mark* which has been altered continues to be descriptive if the mark has been altered only slightly or something has been added to it. Changing the spelling of a word, dividing it, shortening it, adding a syllable, etc. does not give the word distinctiveness except when the word acquires a different meaning or is clearly no longer descriptive. When judging the distinctiveness of the word, attention is given primarily to its meaning in the Finnish and Swedish languages. Its meaning in other major languages, e.g. English, is also considered. Invented words normally possess distinctiveness, as well as existing words that are used in a different meaning.

380. Some early decisions illustrate figure marks which lack distinctiveness or are ordinary geometrical signs that cannot be registered.[1] However, if the mark consists of a picture of the goods, the trademark may become distinctive if the picture is stylised or otherwise peculiar.[2]

1. SAC 1934 II 971 (Ink-stain) a picture resembling an ink-stain lacked distinctiveness.
   SAC 1949 II (Infinity-sign) an infinity-sign in an oval frame lacked distinctiveness.
   SAC 1945 II 169 (Parachute) a trademark for parachutes consisting mainly of pictures of parachutes was not registrable.
2. E.g. SAC 1940 II 118, SAC 1945 II 444.

381. In the following cases trademarks were held to indicate the kind, quality, quantity, use, price, or place or time of manufacture of the goods:

Patent Office[1] *decision of 8 May 1986 (Tetra)*
The trademark 'Tetra' for packaging machines was considered to lack distinctiveness. Because the mark consisted of a generic word that indicates the form of goods and because the word is used in Finland for a certain kind of package, it was not considered to be capable of distinguishing the goods of the applicant from those of others.

SAC 3406/4/95 of 13 June 1995 (Pop-Tarts)
The trademark lacked distinctiveness because it indicated the quality and kind of the product.

SAC 761/4/95 of 17 October 1995 (Super 10)
The word 'super' and '10' both indicated the quality of the cleaner. Also, taken as whole the trademark indicated quality and, since the trademark was not established, it lacked distinctiveness.

SAC 997/4/95 of 21 November 1995 (Finnbind)
A trademark for book binding equipment indicated the origin and use of the goods and services and thus lacked distinctiveness. As it was also not established, the trademark was not registered.

SAC 3064/4/96 of 21 March 1996 (Manager magazin)
The trademark for a magazine consisted of the words 'manager' and 'magazin'. These words indicated kind, quality and target group and thus lacked distinctiveness.

1. Section 51a of the Trade Marks Act provides that the Board of Appeals of the National Board of Patents and Registration serves as the first appeal instance for decisions of the Patent (Trade Mark) Office.

382. Trademarks were held to be distinctive in the following cases:

SC 1977 II 1 (Autophon)
The trademark 'Autophon' for mobile phones and other products was considered distinctive since the word is not part of the common or specialised vocabulary of the Finnish language or of any other language commonly encountered in Finland.

Patent Office[1] decision of 29 April 1986 (Jumbo)
The trademark 'Jumbo' for mobile lifting cranes was held to be distinctive.

1. The Board of Appeals of the National Board of Patents and Registration.

383. Suggestive marks are considered to be distinctive within the meaning of Section 13. Suggestive marks form associations with the goods or with some qualities of them. Such words as 'Aristocrat' and 'Ambassador' give an impression of high quality goods, while 'Facit' for calculators and 'Revelj' for alarm clocks suggest the kind of goods to which they refer. However, the distinction between a descriptive and suggestive mark is blurred, and there are no absolutely clear rules concerning which marks may be registered and which may not.

384. The *place of manufacture* refers to geographical names, including countries, districts, towns, smaller localities, etc. Adjectives indicating the place of manufacture, such as 'Finnish', 'Tropical', etc., are also not registrable. Smaller localities abroad that are not commonly known as the place of manufacture may be registered. Smaller localities in Finland are normally not registrable but such names as those of estates and farms are registrable as well as names like 'Mont Blanc' or 'Etna', where manufacturing is not possible.[1]

1. SOU 1958:10 p. 272.

385. Even though a trademark may at first be descriptive, it may later acquire distinctiveness through use. In such cases the trademark gets a *secondary meaning* in addition to the original meaning of the word. By using the trademark, the target group may, as time passes, regard it as the distinctive mark of a manufacturer. Similarly, a figure that lacks distinctiveness, may acquire it through use and thus become registrable. To acquire such a secondary meaning the mark does not have to be as widely known as a trademark which has become established.[1] It should be noted that even though Section 13 concerns only registered trademarks, established trademarks must also be distinctive in order to acquire protection.

1. P.-L. Haarmann p. 160.

386. The *impediments to registration* are stipulated in Section 14. The first three subparagraphs provide for absolute impediments, whereas subparagraphs 4 to 9 are relative, i.e. the trademark may be registered with the consent of the person whose right is concerned, provided that such registration does not contravene the two first provisions of Section 14.

387. Section 14 provides that:

'A trademark shall not be registered:
1. if it is contrary to law and order, or to morality;
2. if it is liable to mislead the public;
3. if, without proper permission, it incorporates national armorial bearings, a national flag or emblem, a sign or hallmark indicating control and warranty used by the State for goods of the same or a similar type as those for which the trademark is requested, the armorial bearings of a Finnish commune, or the flag, the armorial bearings or other emblem, name or abbreviation of a name which is liable to be confused with the said symbols or emblems, marks, names or abbreviations;
...'

388. The first impediment to registration might be applied, for example, where a trademark is religiously offensive or indecent. A trademark is liable to mislead the public if it gives a false impression of the origin, qualities, etc. of the goods. The second impediment has also been applied in rather few cases. For example, the trademarks 'Finnwheeler' for a Swedish applicant, 'Scandia stimulus' for an applicant from the Bahamas and 'Denver' for a Finnish applicant were not registered.

SAC 1991 A 98 (Voimix)
The trademark 'Voimix' (voi = butter) for a margarine product containing a substantial proportion of butter was not liable to mislead the public as to the quality of the product.

389. The following impediments are relative, i.e. registration may be granted even though the trademark contravenes the provision set out in subparagraphs 4 to 9, provided that the person whose right is concerned consents thereto. However, the trademark may not be registered if it contravenes the provisions set out in subparagraphs 1 to 3 (Sect. 14, para. 2). For example where a new trademark is identical or similar to a prior mark for identical or similar products, the new trademark is not registrable even if the holder of the prior mark agrees to such registration, where the mark is liable to mislead the public as to the commercial origin of the goods. The only exemption is where the applicant is the subsidiary of the holder of the prior mark, or *vice versa*.[1]

SAC 5444/55/84 of 30 April 1985 (Thermax)
The trademark 'Thermax' for construction equipment was not registered because it was identical to the existing and registered trademark 'Thermax' for goods of the

same kind. Even though such registration was accepted by the former holder of the same mark, the new registration was refused, since it would have misled the public as to the commercial origin of the goods.[2]

> '...4. if it is composed of or contains anything that is likely to give the impression of being the protected trade name of another or the subsidiary company name or secondary symbol of another referred to in the third paragraph of Section 3, or of being the name or likeness of another person, unless such name or likeness plainly refers to someone who died a long time ago;
> 5. if it is composed of or contains anything that is likely to give the impression of being the title of the protected literary or artistic work of another person, whenever such work is of original character, or if it constitutes an infringement of the copyright held by another person in such a work or of his right to a photographic illustration;
> 6. if it is liable to be confused with the name or protected trade name of another trader or with a subsidiary company or secondary symbol of the kind referred to in the third paragraph of Section 3, or with the trademark of another which has been registered on the basis of an earlier application, or with the trade symbol of another party that is already established at the time when registration is sought; or
> 7. if it is liable to be confused with a trade symbol being used by another party for his goods at the time of the application, and if the applicant has cognisance of such use at the time of his application and had not used his own mark before the other trade symbol came into use; or
> 8. if it is liable to be confused with a trademark protected by international registration valid in Finland and the date under paragraph 1 of Section 56c granted by the International Bureau is earlier than the date on which registration is sought; or
> 9. if it is liable to be confused with a Community Trademark under paragraph 1 of Section 57 that has been registered on the basis of an earlier application.'

1. P.-L. Haarmann p. 162.
2. L. Drockila p. 93.

390. Subparagraph 4 concerns a trademark that is likely to give the impression of being the name, protected trade name, etc. of another. Where the trademark is not likely to be associated with the name, protected trade name, etc. of another, it is registrable. Note that the use of a trademark including a name, a trade name, a subsidiary company name, etc. is prohibited under Section 3, paragraph 3, unless these lack distinguishing power or the branches of trade or kind of goods concerned are different or the trademark is also the name of the applicant. The name or the picture of a person long since deceased may be registered.

SAC No. 3861 of 15 October 1976 (Markoff)
The trademark 'Alexandra de Markoff' was not registrable, because 'Markoff' was a Finnish surname.

SAC No. 3862 of 15 October 1976 (Goddard)
The registration of the trademark 'Goddard' could not be refused on the grounds that it was likely to give the impression of the name of another person, since the name was not used in Finland and was not so well known in Finland that it would have given the impression of being the name of another person.

391. Subparagraph 6 of Section 14 provides that where a trademark is liable to be confused with the registered or established trademark of another, the trademark is not registrable. The same applies when a trademark is liable to be confused with a name, a trade name, a subsidiary company or secondary symbol. It might be noted that design rights do not constitute grounds for refusal.[1]

SC 1990:53 (Palmroth)
The plaintiff had used his surname 'Palmroth' as a trademark for shoes in the form 'Pertti Palmroth'. 'Pertti Palmroth' had become an established mark. The Court held that consumers and non-specialised traders did not know that goods bearing the marks 'Pertti Palmroth' and 'Juhani Palmroth Jr' were of differing commercial origin. The use of the latter as a mark infringed the rights of the plaintiff to use the established mark, because the surname so dominated the mark that the different first name and the 'Jr' were not sufficient to distinguish the marks from each other.

1. B. Kolster & A. Baltscheffsky & K.-H. Henn p. 65.

392. Subparagraph 7 provides that for a prior mark to be protected against the registration of a new mark it is sufficient that the prior mark has been used and the applicant has cognisance of such use. It is not required that the prior mark be registered or established, nor is it required that it be used in Finland.

SAC 1971 A II 96 (Sperina)
A trademark which had been used abroad was held to have been used within the meaning of Section 14, subparagraph 7 of the Trademarks Act.

393. Establishment. A trademark may also acquire protection by becoming established. Section 2, paragraph 3 provides that a trade symbol is to be regarded as established if it has become generally known in the appropriate business or consumer circles in Finland as a symbol specific to the goods of its proprietor. Establishment is acquired simply by using the trade symbol in question in professional activities. The use may consist, for example, of labelling the goods sold with the symbol or sometimes even simply by using the symbol in a major advertising campaign.

394. Normally a trademark must be used for several years before becoming established. This period may, however, be shortened by marketing campaigns, etc. By effective advertising a trademark may even become established before the goods concerned enter the market.

395. For a symbol to be established it must (1) be generally known, (2) in the appropriate business, (3) in Finland, (4) as a symbol specific to the proprietor's goods. The symbol must be 'generally known', which does not mean that everybody or almost everybody has to know it. Instead of only using the diffuse definition 'generally known' in deciding whether a trademark is established or not, independent market research is used. In Swedish practice it appears that a symbol is generally known when 50 per cent of the relevant target group knows it. It can be argued that where the target group is very large, a smaller percentage, e.g. 30 per cent, should suffice for establishment.[1]

1. L. Pehrson p. 158.

396. The symbol must be generally known within the appropriate business. The appropriate business consists of the target group to which the goods or services concerned are marketed. In addition to the target group, the appropriate business also comprises distributors, wholesalers, importers, etc. For very specialised goods or services, the target group may be limited to only a small group, whereas it may comprise a large proportion of the population in the country when it concerns everyday products such as margarine or toothpaste, etc.[1]

1. B.S. Lassen pp. 196–197.

397. The symbol must be known in Finland. It is of no significance that the symbol is widely known abroad when determining whether it is established in Finland. Nevertheless the symbol may have been made generally known in Finland through advertising in foreign magazines which are commonly read in Finland. The symbol does not have to be known throughout Finland, but it is sufficient that it is generally known in some part of the country. In such a case the trademark will acquire protection only in that part of the country. However, where a mark has acquired protection in any part of the country, it cannot be registered by anybody other than the proprietor of the established mark.[1]

1. SOU 1958:10 p. 221.

398. The trademark must be known as the symbol, name or commercial mark of the goods or services in question. The target group must know that the proprietor uses the symbol to individualise and distinguish his goods or services from those of others, but it is not necessary that the name of the proprietor is known. For the symbol to be able to individualise the goods in question, it must be distinctive.

399. A trademark loses its protection if it ceases to be established. Establishment must be regarded to have ceased if any of the four conditions for establishment described above are no longer fulfilled. This happens, for example, where the trademark has not been used over a long period of time or where the symbol is no longer regarded as the mark of the goods of a certain manufacturer, i.e. it has become degenerate.

Trademarks, Ch. 4

§4. Formalities (Procedure for Acquiring Protection, Establishing and Maintaining Trademarks)

400. Protection for trademarks may be acquired either through registration or through right of establishment, or in both ways. The terms of protection are equal for registered and established trademarks but protection is easier and faster to acquire through registration. As explained above, trademarks which cannot be represented graphically may become protected only through establishment and trademarks that at first lack distinctiveness may later become distinctive through use, thus acquiring protection.

401. Registration. The National Board of Patents and Registration of Finland (hereinafter referred to as the Authority) is the authority which processes trademark registration and maintains the Register of Trademarks in Finland. An application for registration must be submitted to the Authority in writing.[1] It must include the name or trade name of the applicant, the goods and classes of goods for which the mark is intended, the mark itself and, in the case of an applicant not domiciled in Finland, the name and address of a representative in Finland (the trademark agent) (Sects. 17 and 31).[2] Each trademark to be registered requires a separate application.[3]

1. The use of a standardised form prepared by the Authority is recommended, even though it is not compulsory.
2. Sections 17 and 31 of the Trademarks Act.
3. Section 8 of the Trademarks Decree No. 296 of 29 May 1964.

402. A trademark may be registered in one or more classes of goods or services. There are 42 classes, most of which are divided into subclasses.[1] The goods in question must always be stated in the application. An applicant may apply for protection in the whole class (or classes) or only in some of the subclasses. The classification system is of no significance when deciding whether goods are of identical or similar kind as provided in Section 6, and therefore the system is of minor importance for the scope of protection enjoyed by the trademark. It is more important for administrative purposes.[2] The fee depends on the number of classes for which the trademark will be registered, but it does not depend on the subclasses. The filing fee must be paid when the application is filed (Sect. 17, subpara. 2).

1. Section 16 of the Trademarks Act, Decision No. 510 of the National Board of Patents and Registration issued on 16 May 1983 concerning classification of registered trademarks.
2. B.S. Lassen p. 134.

403. Where some element of a trademark cannot be registered, for example, when a trademark consists of a picture and words and the words lack distinctiveness, the trademark cannot acquire protection as whole. In such a case, the part that is not registrable, e.g. the words, may be specifically disclaimed from the protection. If the excluded part later becomes registrable, a fresh registration application may be filed to cover the part (Sect. 16).

404. An applicant seeking to gain priority based on an earlier application for a trademark filed in another country, pursuant to the Paris Convention for the

Protection of Industrial Property or the Agreement Establishing the World Trade Organisation, must file an application within six months of the original application.[1] If the applicant wishes to gain priority then the Authority must be notified of this wish within one month of the date of filing of the application in Finland.[2] Section 57a contains provisions concerning priority with regard to the Community Trademark.

1. Sections 18 and 30 of the Trademarks Act, Sect. 17 of the Trademarks Decree.
2. Section 17 of the Trademarks Decree.

405. An applicant may register a trademark in Finland even though he conducts no business in Finland. In principle, the applicant must present a so-called Certificate of Home State, whereby the applicant demonstrates that he has had the same trademark registered for the same goods in the foreign country in which he carries on his business or where he is domiciled, or of which he is a national (Sect. 28, para. 1). However, on a reciprocal basis, such certificates are normally not required.[1]

1. P.-L. Haarmann p. 176.

406. Section 29 contains the *telle quelle*-rule. It provides that a trademark registered abroad may be registered on a reciprocal basis in Finland as such, provided that such registration does not contravene Section 13 or 14 and that the trademark has not lost its distinguishing power.

407. An application for registration is examined by the Authority prior to registration. The Authority examines whether the application complies with the formal regulations governing applications, whether it meets the requirements for distinctiveness, whether there are impediments as provided in Section 14, whether the prospective trademark is in conflict with registered or established trademarks or with pending applications, and whether it meets the other requirements for registration (Sect. 19). This examination by the Authority is diligent and precise, and in practice provides considerable certainty as to the lawfulness of the registration, while mistakes are rare.[1] In 1993 the average time taken for the examination was 15 months, while the corresponding period in 1997 was 11 months. The Authority also conducts preliminary searches upon request and payment of a separate fee.

1. M. Koktvedgaard & M. Levin p. 302.

408. If the Authority finds that the application cannot be approved for some reason, then it is dismissed *ex officio*. However, prior to rejection the applicant is advised of any obstacles to registration and may submit a statement or rectify the application within a specified period. If the Authority still considers the application unacceptable, then it must be rejected unless there is cause to set a new time limit (Sect. 19, para 2).

409. After approving an application, the Authority registers the trademark and issues public notice thereof. Any third parties may notify their opposition to the registration by filing an opposition submission within two months of the date of the

Trademarks, Ch. 4

public notice, after which the applicant is allowed a time period for submitting a statement. An opposition submission may be examined even if it has been withdrawn (Sect. 20).[1] If an obstacle to registration is found, then the Authority must revoke the registration (Sect. 21). Otherwise the registration takes effect as from the date on which the application was filed.

1. Before 1996 a trademark was registered after the two month period for opponents. Now the procedure complies with the procedure in EPC.

410. A final decision by the Authority may be appealed by the applicant or by the opponent if the decision has been unfavourable for that party (Sect. 51). The appeal must be filed with the Board of Appeal at the National Board of Patents and Registration of Finland within 60 days of the day on which the appellant was notified of the decision.[1] The decision of the Board of Appeal is open to further appeal to the Supreme Administrative Court within 60 days of the latter decision.

1. Section 51a of the Trademarks Act, Sect. 4 of the Act No. 576 of 26 June 1992 on the Appeal Procedure for Decisions by the National Board of Patents and Registration.

411. The National Board of Patents and Registration also takes charge of duties in Finland relating to the international registration of trademarks pursuant to the Madrid Protocol of 27 June 1989 (Sect. 53).

412. An application regarding a Community Trademark may be lodged with the National Board of Patents and Registration, which forwards such applications to the Community Trademark Office in Alicante (Sect. 57).

413. Establishment. The other way to acquire protection is through right of establishment. A trademark is established when it has become generally known in the relevant business circles in Finland as a symbol specific to the goods of its proprietor (Sect. 3). No formalities are required for a trademark to be established. A more detailed analysis of the requirements for establishment is given in §3 above.

414. Maintaining trademarks. Once a trademark has been registered, the registration continues to be effective for ten years from the date of registration. Any renewal must be submitted in writing if the proprietor seeks to amend the registration. Otherwise renewals are effected by paying the renewal fee. A renewal may be submitted no earlier than one year before and no later than six months after the registration expires (Sect. 22). A registration may be forfeit if the mark has not been used during the preceding five years (Sect. 26).[1]

1. See §8 for requirements of use.

415. An established trademark acquires protection through establishment if it meets the requirements for so doing imposed by Section 2. Normally this means that the trademark is protected for as long as it remains in use. If a registered trademark has become established during a period when it has been registered, then it will be protected by establishment even after its registration has expired.

§5. Ownership and Transfer (Assignment – Licences)

416. The ownership and transfer of trademarks is basically a matter of general Finnish property law, but there are some special provisions in the Trademarks Act. Title to a trademark is acquired by the person in whose name it is registered or has become established. An employee does not normally acquire the right to a trademark, but the trademark instead belongs to the 'business'.[1] Before 1993 only an entrepreneur could acquire a trademark, but since this time anybody has been able to acquire a trademark for goods and services purveyed in business.

    1. M. Koktvedgaard & M. Levin p. 319.

417. In many cases an agent or representative has registered or established the trademark of a principal whose products or services the agent sells pursuant to a distribution agreement or similar contractual relationship. If the parties have not agreed about who retains title to the trademark upon termination of the contract, then the trademark is transferred to the principal. Therefore, and since the establishment of a trademark on a new market often requires significant investments by the agent, it must be noted that the legal situation of the agent is dependent upon these contractual arrangements.

418. Title to a trademark may be transferred to another party and the transfer may cover either all or only a part of the goods for which the trademark is protected. Unless otherwise agreed, a trademark accompanies the property when a firm changes hands. The previous and the new owner may also agree that they use the same mark for different kinds of goods (Sect. 32).

419. The transfer of a mark may be registered in the trademarks register. If the registering authority finds that the assignment of the mark is clearly liable to mislead the public, then registration will be withheld until the mark has been altered to eliminate the fault. Registration has no effects on the relationship between the parties. However, a transfer that has not been entered in the register does not affect a third party who, in good faith, has acquired title to the trademark (Sect. 33).[1]

    1. Note that Swedish Trademarks Act differs at this point. *See also* B. Godenhielm, 'Om godtrosskydd inom immaterialrätten', NIR No. 1, 1996.

420. A trademark may be mortgaged. For such a mortgage to be effective it must be made in writing and registered. No right to a mortgage exists before the agreement is registered. Only a trademark upon which a mortgage has been established can be subject to distraint. If the property of the proprietor of a trademark is divested on bankruptcy, then the trademark is included in the bankrupt's estate (Sects. 33 and 35). A trademark may also be inherited.

421. A trademark may also be licenced. The licence may concern either all or part of the goods covered by the trademark, it may concern the whole of the country or some part thereof, and it may be exclusive or non-exclusive. A licensee may not assign the licence or grant sub-licences without permission. The licence

Trademarks, Ch. 4

may be registered with similar effects as apply when registering the assignment of a trademark. The registering authority may withhold registration if it finds that assignment of the mark is clearly liable to mislead the public (Sect. 34). There are no specific rules in Finland concerning franchise agreements and thus the provisions in the Trademarks Act may become applicable to such agreements.

§6. SCOPE OF EXCLUSIVE RIGHTS

422. The central content of the protection consists in the right to prohibit others from using a similar symbol. Section 4, paragraph 1 provides that no person other than the proprietor of the protected trademark may use for his goods any symbol liable to be confused with it.[1] The mark may not be used on the goods or their packaging, in advertising, in commercial documents or in any other way, including orally. Furthermore, the goods of another marked with a symbol which is protected in Finland, or with a symbol which is liable to be confused with it may not be imported.[2] Normally only symbols for identical or similar kinds of goods may be regarded as leading to confusion (Sect. 6, para. 1). Protection may, however, be extended to apply to other kinds of goods as well (Sect. 6, para. 2).[3]

1. *See* §10 for remedies and sanctions for infringements of Sect. 4.
2. *See also* §7 for a discussion of exhaustion of rights.
3. Section 6, para. 2:
   'Notwithstanding paragraph 1, the confusability of symbols **may** be referred to in favour of any symbol which has a reputation in this country, if the use of a symbol of another without due cause would take unfair advantage of, or be detrimental to the distinctive character or repute of the earlier mark.'

423. Section 7 provides that if there are several parties demanding sole rights to trade symbols bearing confusing similarity, then the party which can demonstrate the earliest entitlement must be given preference. The relevant date concerning entitlement is the date of filing of the documents for registration or the date on which the mark became established. However, Sections 8 and 9 provide two exemptions from the rule in Section 7: the rules of preclusion and passivity. These are discussed in greater detail in §7 below.

424. Registration of trademarks is a formality so that initially there is no obligation for their proprietors to actually use them.[1] Companies do often register several 'defensive' trademarks in order to broaden the scope of protection enjoyed by the mark. Defensive marks are not used by these companies for their goods and are not even intended for future use. However, by registering 'Vestolen', for example, the proprietor of the registered trademark 'Vestol' ensures that a competitor may neither use nor register 'Vestolen' for similar kinds of goods.

1. However, Sect. 26, para. 2 provides that the registration shall be forfeited if the mark has not been used over the preceding five years and the proprietor is unable to supply an acceptable reason for this. *See* §8 for requirements of use.

425. Trademarks are liable to be confused with one another when some likelihood of confusion exists concerning the commercial origin of goods or services. In order to establish that a mark is liable to be confused, it is sufficient that the mark is potentially confused with another which is registered or protected by establishment. However, even if two trademarks are identical they are not liable to be confused if they apply to different kinds of goods. Therefore, it must be established which kinds of goods are identical or similar within the meaning of Section 6.

426. The Patent Office uses an international classification of goods and services for the purposes of registration. Goods are divided into 34 classes and services into 8 classes, and most of the classes are further divided into several subclasses. A class may include the same kinds of goods but also entirely different kinds of goods. By contrast, almost the same kinds of products may be registered under two different classes. Trademarks may be registered in one or more of these classes or subclasses (Sect. 16). However, the classification system is mainly for registration purposes. When considering whether the goods are of identical or similar kind, their classification is of little significance.[1]

1. P.-L. Haarmann p. 167.

427. Relevant criteria when establishing whether goods or services are of a similar kind are raw materials, the use of the goods, the applicable marketing and distribution systems and the target group.[1] The goods are similar if, in the case of two trademarks which are liable to be confused, the consumers associate the goods with the same [common] commercial origin. Sometimes goods may be considered to be similar even though they are used for diametrically opposite purposes. Ultimately the decision concerning the similarity in kind of goods or services is made *in casu.*
Two judgments of the Supreme Administrative Court are set out below:

SAC 1966 A II 125 (Esquire)
The trademark 'Esquire' was not registered for shoes because the same word was already registered for socks.
SAC No. 655 of 15 February 1971 (Bali)
The registered trademark 'Bally' for shoes etc. did not constitute an obstacle to registering the trademark 'Bali' for brassieres because the goods were not of identical or similar kind.

1. A. Siponen p. 29, L. Drockila pp. 191*ff.*

428. Furthermore, it must be established whether a trademark is liable to be confused with another trademark.[1] There are two main rules when considering whether there is a risk of confusion between two marks. (1) The marks should not be compared side by side. Instead, it is more important that the marks are liable to be confused by an average consumer in the target group in a potential buying situation. (2) Purchasers do not usually see the trademarks side by side in a buying situation, but they have only a weak recollection of the other mark, and therefore their overall impression of the marks is decisive.[2] Mere differences in some details are usually not enough to relieve the confusion.

Trademarks, Ch. 4

1. Note that the proprietor of a mark may register marks which are liable to be confused with his own marks.
2. V. Tiili (1987) p. 703.

429. The kind of goods and the target group are also important. Trademarks for everyday commodities are more likely to be confused than trademarks for expensive products such as motor vehicles, to which considerable attention is paid when purchasing. Well known brand names for high quality products are less likely to be confused than marks for mass products. Also, marks for specialist products are less likely to be confused than those for everyday consumer products.[1]

1. A. Siponen p. 34.

430. Trademarks are often divided into strong and weak marks. Strong marks are often invented words, pictures with a high degree of distinctiveness or other marks which are very distinctive. Weak marks consist often, for example, of suggestive or somehow descriptive words, of a simple geometrical figure or of letters. The protection of weak marks against confusable marks is weaker and not as broad as the protection of strong marks. However, through use a mark originally considered to be weak may become strong and thus acquire broader and stronger protection.[1]

1. E.g. SC 1987:11 (Adidas). The simple geometrical figure consisting of three parallel stripes on sporting shoes had obtained a strong protection through its use over a 20 year period.

431. When deciding whether trademarks consisting of words are liable to be confused, attention must be paid to the pronunciation, appearance and meaning of the words. Normally, even if only part of a trademark is open to confusion, then the entire mark is held to be so open. However, where a mark contains a common suffix, such as -mycin, -derm, -tronic, -lon, -text, etc., the first part is more important when considering whether the marks are liable to confusion.[1]

1. A. Siponen p. 35.

432. Some judgments concerning confusion from the Supreme Court, the Supreme Administrative Court and the Board of Appeal of the National Board of Patents and Registration (NBPR) are set out below:

SC 1967 II 108	'Kortaspin'	=	'Aspirin'
	'Kodaspin'	=	'Cafaspin'
	'Primaspin'	=	'Bonaspin'[1]
SC 1985 II 85	'Einolan'	=	'Kleinol'
	'Einola'	=	'Cleinol'
SAC 1974 A II 122	'Flour du Roi'	=	'Flor du Region'
SAC 1970 A II 150	'Sartor'	≠	'Sanfor'
SAC 67/4/96	'Enfa'	=	'Infa'
SAC 867/4/93	'Ascotel'	≠	'Alcatel'
SAC 3836/4/95	'Contourelle'	≠	'Contour', 'Lady Contour'[2]
SAC 1971	'Blondys'	≠	'Blondex', 'Blondor'[3]

SAC No. 472 1993	'Wake Up'	≠	'Seven Up', '7 Up'
NBPR 170/T/94	'Comtesse du Barry'	=	'Comtesse', 'Comtess'
NBPR 134/T/94	'Basie'	≠	'Bass'
NBPR 183/T/94	'Tempur'	≠	'Tempus'
NBPR 166/T/94	'Esta'	≠	'Asta'
NBPR 236/T/94	'Aristoc Toners'	≠	'Body Toners'
NBPR decision of 26 March 1985	'Märklin'	≠	'Merlin'

1. The strong suffix 'spin' was protected.
2. See V. Tiili & P.-L. Aro who refer to SAC praxis.
3. Weak protection because 'blond' is suggestive.

433. Visual similarity is most important when considering the confusion of figure marks. In the case of other marks, the overall impression made by the mark is decisive. Sometimes, where the motive is characteristic, it may also be protected, the dog listening to a gramophone in 'His Masters Voice', for example. However, where the figure is common, e.g. a geometrical figure, the mark enjoys only weak protection. When a figure mark is registered in colour, the colour may either increase or reduce the risk of confusion. If a mark is registered in black and white, then the protection extends to all colours.

SC 1987:11 (Adidas)
In the Adidas case, the Supreme Court held that the mark used for Adidas shoes and consisting of three parallel stripes enjoyed protection by right of establishment and that a competitor was prohibited from using a mark for shoes consisting of four parallel stripes. Even though the mark was a simple geometrical figure, and as such was a weak mark which probably at first lacked distinctiveness and thus could not have been registered, it had, through use over a 20 year period acquired strong protection.[1] It was established that the Adidas mark was widely known among the target group. The Court held that the overall impression of the competitor's mark was similar to that of the Adidas mark and, in consequence, that a consumer might, based on impressions obtained from the Adidas mark, believe that the competitor's products were Adidas products.

1. V. Tiili (1987) p. 701.

434. Section 6, paragraph 2 provides for an exemption from the rule that trademarks can lead to confusion only if they apply to identical or similar kind of goods.[1] This has its origin in the old Kodak doctrine, but its application is much broader. It provides that

> 'the confusability of symbols may be referred to in favour of a symbol which has a reputation in this country, if the use of a symbol of another without due cause would mean taking unfair advantage of, or being detrimental to, the distinctive character or the repute of the earlier mark.'

Section 6, paragraph 3 provides that the same applies to subsidiary companies and secondary symbols.

1. Section 6, para. 2 was amended by Act No. 39 of 21 January 1993.

435. The Trademarks Act was amended in 1993 so as to harmonise it with Articles 4 and 5 of the Trademarks Directive.[1] Under the provisions of the old Act, the requirements which had to be met in order for Section 6, paragraph 2 to apply were much more strict.

1. First Council Directive 89/104 of 21 December 1988.

436. For a mark to acquire protection against another mark not applicable to an identical or similar kind of goods, it is necessary that the prior mark has a reputation in Finland.[1] The better known the mark is, the more it is established and the stronger is its protection against confusing marks.[2] Furthermore, for Section 6, paragraph 2 to apply, the use of the confusing symbol must take unfair advantage of the distinctiveness and goodwill of the prior mark, or the use of the other symbol must be detrimental to the distinctiveness or goodwill of the prior mark. The target groups for the goods marked with the trademarks must overlap at least partially.[3]

1. Note that reputation in only some parts does not suffice, and it is required that the mark is known throughout the country.
2. Government Bill 1992/302.
3. M. Koktvedgaard & M. Levin pp. 343–344.

437. There have been no judgments concerning the application of the new Section 6, paragraph 2. A judgment made under the old Act is set out below:

SAC 1985 A II 145 (Rolls-Royce)
The trademark 'Rolls-Royce', of which the abbreviated form 'Rolls' was also used, had been very effectively established and was widely known in Finland. The use of the mark 'Roll's', which was essentially similar to 'Rolls-Royce', for clothing and shoes would have taken unfair advantage of the reputation and value of 'Rolls-Royce'.

SAC No. 3156 of 25 August 1977 (Marabo)
The registered and established trademark 'Marabou' for chocolate was not held to be an obstacle to the registration of 'Marabo' for contraceptives. 'Marabou' was not considered to have been strongly established and the registering of 'Marabo' was not held to be detrimental to the reputation and goodwill of 'Marabou'.

§7. Limitation of the Scope of Trademark Protection

438. Exhaustion. Until recently in Finnish law, trademarks have been considered to be internationally exhausted. However, in 1995 the Trademarks Act was harmonised with Article 7 of the Trademarks Directive by adding a new Section 10a. Section 10a, paragraph 1 provides that the rights conferred by a trademark are exhausted for goods which have been put on the market within the European Economic Area (EEA).[1] Section 10a provides that:

> 'The proprietor of a trademark may not forbid the use of the trademark in goods that the proprietor or some other person with his consent has, using this trademark, put on the market within the territory of the European Economic Area.'

1. Note that Art. 7 of the Trademarks Directive concerns only the European Communities.

439. This accords with the free movement of goods and means that, with reference to trademark rights, no one may prohibit the importation of goods where these goods have been put on the market within the EEA with the proprietor's consent. Thus, nowadays the principle of territorial exhaustion is applied in Finland and is considered to exclude the principle of global exhaustion.[1] Consequently, parallel importation is no longer allowed from outside of the EEA.

1. Government Bill 1995/135 p. 14. There has been much debate about this and this view has been criticised.

440. Even though parallel importation is allowed within the EEA, the importer is not allowed to use the logotype of the protected mark in marketing the goods, to repackage the goods or to otherwise give the impression of being an authorised dealer in the goods.[1] He may only display the goods, use pictures of them in marketing and so on.[2] Section 10a, paragraph 2 provides that paragraph 1 does not apply if the proprietor has justified grounds to oppose putting the goods on the market in Finland, especially if the goods have been altered or have deteriorated. Where the goods have been put on market without the proprietor's consent, the proprietor may prohibit the use of the mark on those goods in Finland, regardless of where the goods have been put on the market.

SC 1990:49 (Jackpot)
The parent company of the proprietor of the established trademark 'Jackpot' had rescinded the supply agreement with its foreign sub-supplier and notified that goods which had been manufactured by the sub-supplier and which were marked with the protected mark were at the disposal of the sub-suppliers. In doing so, the parent company had not given its consent to putting the goods on the market. Therefore, the importer of the goods infringed the trademark rights of the proprietor by importing the goods to Finland.

1. However, repackaging of medicines has been allowed in recent EC law practice. *See* cases C-427/93, C-429/93, C-436/93, C-71/94, C-72/94, C-73/94 and C-232/94.
2. M. Koktvedgaard & M. Levin pp. 324*ff.*

441. Individual surname, address and trade name. The proprietor of a protected mark cannot, in principle, prohibit another from using his own surname, address or trade name as a trademark unless this is liable to cause confusion (Sect. 3, para. 1). The same applies to a subsidiary company and to a secondary symbol. However,

Trademarks, Ch. 4

where the surname, etc. is used in a manner contrary to good business practice, its use as a trademark may be prohibited under the Unfair Trade Practices Act.[1]

1. Act No. 1061 of 22 December 1978.

442. The proprietor of a mark may not prohibit another from the fair use of a word indicating the *kind, quantity, quality, use, price or place or time of manufacture* of the goods. However, such a word may not be used in a manner which is contrary to good business practice, or otherwise be used in a way which is misleading as to commercial or geographical origin. Section 13 provides that such words may not be registered as trademarks. However, they may become protected through right of establishment.

443. *Spare parts, etc.* Section 4, paragraph 2 provides that if spare parts, accessories or the like, which are suitable for use with the goods of another, are offered for sale, then it is illegal to allude to the trade symbol of such other party in any manner liable to create the impression that the goods originate with the proprietor of the said symbol or that the proprietor has permitted the use of the symbol. This is an important rule which allows independent manufacturers of spare parts to market their goods as '... suitable for ...' the products of another, e.g. BMW, IBM, etc.[1] However, the manufacturers of spare parts, etc. may not, for example, use the registered logo-types or figures of another.[2]

1. P.-L. Haarmann p. 171.
2. L. Pehrson p. 339.

444. *Comparative advertising.* The protected mark of another may be used in comparative marketing. The comparison must be correct and true and the marketing must meet the requirements imposed by the Unfair Trade Practices Act.[1]

SC 1956 II 90 (Volkswagen)
Spare parts for Volkswagen had been sold in packages marked with the registered trademark of 'Volkswagen' even though the manufacturer was not entitled to use the mark. The manufacturer was prohibited from continuing to sell the goods in such packages and was obliged to label the packages clearly with a mark indicating the manufacturer.

1. Unfair Trade Practices Act No. 1061 of 22 December 1978.

445. *Preclusion and passivity.* There are two exemptions from the rule in Section 7 that priority to a trademark must be given to the person who can claim the earliest entitlement. The *preclusion-rule* concerns situations where a registered trademark which has been used in Finland for a period of five successive years is liable to be confused with an earlier registered or established mark. Section 8 provides that the use of the later mark shall not be prohibited, provided that the application for registration was made in good faith and that the proprietor of the earlier mark had been aware of such use of the later mark for such a period. This means that the proprietor of the earlier mark must prohibit the use of a later mark within five years of the registration or otherwise lose his right to prohibit the other from

using the later mark. Note that for the later mark to acquire protection from prohibition, it must be used for five years. Registration alone is not sufficient.

446. The *passivity-rule* concerns situations where an established trademark is liable to be confused with an earlier established or registered trademark. Section 9 provides that if the proprietor of the earlier mark has not subsequently taken steps to prevent the use of the later trademark within a reasonable period of time, then he shall no longer be entitled to prohibit the use of the later trademark. The reasonable period of time depends mainly on the extent to which the mark has been used and on whether the proprietor of the later mark has acted in good faith.[1]

1. P.-L. Haarmann p. 160.

447. For Sections 8 or 9 to be applied there must be two trademarks on the market which are liable to be confused with one another. Section 10 provides that in such cases the Court may decide that one or both of the marks may be used only in a specific manner, for example when shaped in a particular way or with the addition of a place name or another feature.

448. Finally, it may be noted that the exclusive right to a trademark extends only to marks used for goods or services offered for sale or otherwise purveyed in business. This means that trademarks may, for example, be collected (in the same way as postage stamps, for example) or that they may be included in a book about trademarks without infringing their associated rights.[1]

1. M. Koktvedgaard & M. Levin p. 345.

§8. USE REQUIREMENTS

449. No immediate use requirement exists in Finnish trademark law. Trademarks may be registered by a formal procedure and there is no requirement for the applicant to use or to start using the trademark. A trademark may be registered even if the applicant has absolutely no intention to use it at the time or in the future.

450. Nevertheless, once a trademark has been registered, Section 26, paragraph 2 provides that it may be forfeited if it has not been used during the preceding five years and the proprietor is unable to provide an acceptable reason for such failure to use. The five year period is counted from the date of registration or from the date when the trademark was used for the last time.[1]

1. P. Kolve p. 72.

451. It is not entirely clear what kind of use is considered to be sufficient to interrupt the time period. The sale of the goods or services concerned is normally sufficient. Sometimes an advertising campaign to prepare for the marketing of goods is also sufficient, as, for example, may be a market survey, the display of the goods at trade fairs, etc. However, actions such as a couple of advertisements, offers to customers, etc. effected merely in order to interrupt the period are not sufficient. The mark must have been genuinely used in the sale or marketing of the goods in question. The extent of activities required also depends on the kind of goods. The requirements are more stringent for consumer goods and other goods sold in larger quantities than they are for certain specialist goods. For the latter, the use requirements may be met, for example, by selling a single product over a couple of years. In some cases a trademark may be regarded as used in Finland even where the mark has been advertised in foreign magazines, provided that these are read in Finland.

452. In a Swedish case,[1] the trademark 'Budweiser Budvar' for beer, registered in the name of the Czech company Budvar, was not held to have been used during the time period. The beer had been served (free of charge) at ten professional fairs over the five year period, advertising handouts and openers had been distributed and the company had been involved in negotiations aiming to begin distribution of the beer in Sweden.[2] In another Swedish case, the proprietor of a registered figure had used a slightly different figure. Pursuant to Article 5(c)(2) of the Paris Convention, the Court of Appeal held that the mark had to be considered as having been in use even though the mark which had actually been used was not identical to the registered mark.[3]

1. Supreme Court judgment 1987:5 of 15 January 1987 (Sweden).
2. J. Starell p. 39.
3. P. Kolve p. 78.

453. In Finnish practice common reasons in some businesses, taxation reasons, or purely financial reasons are not acceptable reasons for interrupting the time period. It has been suggested that only reasons of a *force majeure* type and reasons which are unexpected and do not depend on the proprietor may be regarded as acceptable reasons within the meaning of Article 26, paragraph 2.[1]

1. P. Kolve p. 84. However, compare with V. Tiili & P.-L. Aro p. 75.

454. The use of the mark with the proprietor's consent must be regarded as equivalent to its use by the proprietor. Furthermore, Section 26, paragraph 2 provides that a mark cannot be forfeited if it has been used after the expiry of a five year period of non-use, but before the request for forfeiture. No weight is given to use during the last three months before the request was made. Section 26, paragraph 3 provides that a trademark which is registered for many kinds of goods may be forfeited in respect of only some of them.

§9. Duration of Protection – Renewal – Termination

455. The termination of a trademark means that the proprietor loses his exclusive right to the mark, but this alone does not prohibit him from using the mark. Where the mark has become misleading the Court may, however, prohibit its use and if it is registered by another, then it will no longer be possible for the original proprietor to use it.

456. Duration of protection and renewal. Contrary to other intellectual property rights, trademark rights are not restricted in time. An established trademark is protected for as long as the requirements for a symbol to become established are met as explained above in §3. Section 22, paragraph 1 provides that the registration of a trademark continues in force for ten years from the date of registration. The registration may thereafter be renewed an unlimited number of times merely by paying the renewal fee. It may not be renewed sooner than one year before, nor later than six months after the registration expires. If the proprietor chooses to amend the registration, he must request renewal in writing from the registering authority. The proprietor may also request the deletion of the mark from the register.

457. Termination. Invalidity. Section 25 provides that a trademark which has been registered contrary to the provisions of the Trademarks Act is to be declared null and void. Such a trademark may have been registered despite initial obstacles to registration, for example if the trademark was not distinctive at the time of registration (Sect. 13), or may have been contrary to law and order or to morality, liable to mislead the public or in conflict with prior rights (Sect. 14). A trademark may also be declared null and void if it is registered contrary to the requirements imposed by Section 1, for example if it cannot be represented graphically.

458. However, Sections 8 or 9 concerning preclusion and passivity might become applicable where a later mark is in conflict with prior rights. Furthermore, Section 25 provides that an obstacle to registration must still exist at the time when the mark is declared null and void. For example a trademark which initially should not have been registered because of lack of distinctiveness might later become distinctive and thus may no longer be declared null and void.

459. Revocation. A trademark may also be forfeited because of some change in circumstances occurring after registration. Section 26 provides that an exclusive right to a trademark is to be forfeited if the mark has lost its distinctiveness, if it has become misleading or contrary to law and order or to morality, or if the mark has not been used for five years as provided in Section 26, paragraph 2.

460. If a trademark has lost its distinctiveness it is said to have become *degenerate*. Degeneration means that a mark that was once distinctive has, over time, been transformed into a generic or common name used in the trade for a kind of product or service. Consequently, the mark is unable to distinguish between the products of the original proprietor of the mark and those of other suppliers of goods of the same kind and, therefore, the trademark can no longer be protected. Well known examples of degenerated trademarks are, for example, 'Dynamit[e]', 'Jeep' and 'Nylon'.

461. Trademarks which have not become degenerate are always very well established and normally extremely valuable. Therefore the proprietor should take pains to prevent such a trademark from becoming degenerate. The proprietor should not use the trademark as a general type-term for the goods, as an adjective or inflect it in any way. Furthermore, the mark should always be typed in capital letters or in a specific logotype and the proprietor should sometimes also use the generic trade name for the goods in question. Even though the proprietor cannot require newspapers and magazines, for example, to respect his trademark rights, he may invoke Section 11 and require that where a registered trademark is reproduced in dictionaries, glossaries, etc., it is indicated that the mark is registered as such. Normally this is achieved by using the ® sign or the ™ sign, by writing Reg. TM or in some corresponding manner. Trademarks are not prone to become degenerate in the Nordic countries as easily as in the English speaking world.

462. A trademark must also be forfeited if the mark has become *misleading* (Sect. 26, para. 1(2)).[1] A mark may be misleading particularly as to the kind, quality or geographical origin of the goods. A mark may become misleading as to the geographical origin of the goods, for example, where the origin of the goods has changed to one other than that indicated by the mark. Otherwise a trademark may become misleading only in exceptional circumstances.

1. Compare with Sect. 14, para. 1(2).

463. Finally, a trademark which has become *contrary to law and order or to morality*, must be forfeited. This provision is applied only in very exceptional circumstances.

464. Section 27 provides that anyone who suffers inconvenience as a result of a registration may bring an action against the proprietor in Court seeking to have the registration declared invalid or forfeited. If the case is based on Section 26, then the action may also be brought by the public prosecutor or by a body safeguarding the interests of persons carrying on the trade or profession concerned.

§10. INFRINGEMENT AND REMEDIES

465. In cases of infringement, the Trademarks Act provides various kinds of remedies.[1] Section 38 provides that anyone who infringes the right to a protected trademark may be *prohibited by the Court from continuing or repeating the said delinquency* unless there are special reasons to the contrary. This is, in practice, the most important sanction.[2]

1. *See* §6 for a discussion of the scope of exclusive rights and of what constitutes infringements.
2. V. Tiili & P.-L. Aro p. 69.

466. During the proceedings or in its judgment the Court may issue a *temporary injunction* to discontinue the alleged infringement until the judgment has become final. Before such an injunction is issued the proprietor may be ordered to provide sufficient security for any damage the respondent may suffer (Sect. 48). An injunction order may also be requested pursuant to Chapter 7 of the Procedural Code.[1]

1. E. Nordman *et al.* p. 163.

467. Section 38, paragraph 2 provides that if an infringement has been deliberate or has arisen due to negligence, then the injured party is entitled to *compensation* for any *damage* suffered. The damages and compensation to which the proprietor is entitled depend on the degree of culpability of the infringing party. The damages may be adjusted as deemed reasonable if there has been only slight negligence. However, normally it would have been the duty of the infringing party to investigate whether the mark in question was protected, especially where it had been registered. Thus, the infringing party is normally considered to have acted negligently where he has not respected a registered mark. Indemnification consists of compensation for falls in sales, for market damages and for direct losses and costs. In the case of falls in sales, it is the losses of the proprietor which determine the damages, not the profits of the infringing party. Market damages consist, for example, of losses in the goodwill of the mark because of the lower quality of the goods.[1] It is difficult for the courts to estimate the damages in practice. In *SC 1985 II 85 (Einola)* the Court considered the damages to amount to FIM 20,000, in *SC 1990:49 (Carly Gry)* to FIM 50,000 and in *SC 1990:53 (Palmroth)* to FIM 500,000. In Swedish practice damages have normally been estimated to be between SEK 1,000 and 50,000.[2]

1. M. Koktvedgaard & M. Levin pp. 405-407.
2. E. Karlsson p. 390.

468. Even though the respondent did not act in a negligent manner, the infringement may occasion financial consequences. According to Section 38, paragraph 3 the Court may, where deemed reasonable in view of the financial and other circumstances of the respondent, order him to *transfer to the injured party the profits* gained by the infringement for up to the three preceding years.

469. An action seeking damages or claiming the profits gained by the infringement must be brought within three years of the time when the injured party learned of the infringement and of the identity of the delinquent party and, however, no later than ten years after the infringement (Sect. 40, para. 1). In the case of a registered trademark, the injured party may also secure damages for infringements arising before the date of registration. In such cases the action must be filed within a year of the said date (Sect. 40, para. 2).

470. Section 39, paragraph 1 provides that anybody who deliberately infringes the right to a protected trademark is to be sentenced to a *fine* for infringing the right to a trademark. If the infringement is committed in a manner conducive to causing considerable financial losses, then the delinquent party is to be sentenced for an industrial rights offence pursuant to Chapter 49, Section 2 of the Penal Code to a fine or to a term of imprisonment not exceeding two years. Unless requested by the injured party, a prosecution for infringement shall not be brought by the public prosecutor (Sect. 39, para. 2).

471. Section 41, paragraph 1 provides that upon request the Court may order, where reasonable, that symbols which have been placed without authorisation on goods, on their packaging, in documentation, etc., are to be *erased or moved* so that the symbols can no longer be misused. If this is not possible, then the Court may order that the goods so marketed are to be destroyed. Upon request the Court may also order that the goods are to be transferred to the injured party against payment.

472. Section 41, paragraph 2 provides that upon request by the injured party, goods which have been marketed without authorisation using a protected symbol may be *sequestered* by order of the public prosecutor or of the Court. If considered necessary, the injured party may be required to lodge an acceptable security for possible costs and damages caused by such sequestration.

473. Section 42 provides that the District Court of Helsinki is the sole *competent court* in the first instance in all matters concerning the Trademarks Act.[1] An application for an interim injunction, as provided in Section 38, may be heard in criminal proceedings (Sect. 43). Such a measure is usually to be secured more easily, and at an earlier stage, in criminal than in civil proceedings.[2]

    1. Government Bill 1983/37 p. 9.
    2. E. Nordman *et al.* p. 168.

§11. Overlapping and Relation to Other Intellectual Property Laws

474. One of the underlying principles in all Nordic intellectual property legislation is that the various intellectual property rights can and must complement each other. There are no obstacles to the existence of cumulative and parallel rights to the same product, since the various intellectual property rights have different scopes of protection.[1]

    1. M. Levin (1990) p. 170.

475. Registered designs. Pursuant to the Registered Designs Act,[1] a registered design right protects the appearance of an article or ornament. Section 1 of the Act provides that the exclusive right to a design may be acquired through registration. The term 'Design' refers to the prototype of the appearance of an article or ornament and may be two- or three-dimensional. An 'article' is a specific manufactured item *in concreto* and, therefore, design rights cannot be acquired for specific interior designs, tattoos on human beings, etc. The get-up, shape or form of the goods or of their packaging may be protected as a registered design. The same may also be protected by trademark rights and thus the protection provided by registered designs and by trademarks may in some circumstances be overlapping.

    1. Registered Designs Act No. 221 of 12 March 1971 (as amended).

476. Commonly protected designs for goods are, for example, packages and spare parts, especially for cars. As explained above in §7, the holder of a trademark for a car cannot prohibit other manufacturers of spare parts for the car from selling them marked as suitable for the car concerned. However, by registering the design of the spare part, the proprietor may prohibit its manufacture. Ornaments are normally two-dimensional designs used, for example, for decorative purposes.[1] Registered designs are considered more extensively below in Chapter 6.

1. P.-L. Haarmann p. 135.

477. Trade names. Trade names are involved in some of the provisions of the Trademarks Act. Section 3, paragraphs 1 and 2 provide that any person may *inter alia* use his trade name, subsidiary company or secondary symbol as a symbol for his goods, unless this is liable to cause confusion with a protected trademark, a name, an address or a trade name. Section 3, paragraph 3 provides that the trade name of another may not be included in a trademark. Nor may the subsidiary company or secondary symbol of another be included unless these lack distinguishing power or the branches of trade or kinds of goods concerned are different. Furthermore, Section 14, subparagraphs 4 and 6 provide that a trademark may not be registered if it is composed of anything likely to give the impression of being, or likely to be confused with the trade name, subsidiary company or secondary symbol of another.

478. Correspondingly, the trademark of another may not be used as a trade name. Section 14, subparagraph 4 of the *Trade Names Act*[1] provides that a trade name may not, without proper consent, include anything that is liable to be confused with the trademark of another. Moreover, Section 18 provides that the Court may prohibit the use of a trade name which is misleading or contrary to fair trading practice.

1. Trade Names Act No. 128 of 2 February 1979.

479. Finally, sometimes where a symbol, package, furnishing, etc. cannot be protected as a trademark, its use by another may be contrary to the *Unfair Trade Practices Act.*[1] Section 1 of the Act comprises a general clause prohibiting any practice which is contrary to fair trading practice or otherwise unfair towards another trader. The general clause may be applied *inter alia* to slavish imitation. In principle imitation is allowed as long as, for example, the goods are not protected by intellectual property rights. However, if the goods are liable to be confused as to their commercial origin, then imitation is contrary to fair trading practice and thus prohibited. For there to be a risk of confusion, the goods must be distinctive to some extent. Normally there is no risk of confusion if the goods are marked with a trademark, the name of the manufacturer or the like. Concerning identical or similar packages of goods, it has been held that the risk of confusion is not removed simply by marking the packages with one's own mark, but that there must also be other differences as well.[2]

Market Court 1984:8
The colours and their setting on the packages of the respondent were similar to those on the packages of the plaintiff. As a whole, the packages were similar and the only clear difference between them was the trademark on the package of the plaintiff. The Court considered that the packages were liable to be confused as to

Trademarks, Ch. 4

the commercial origin of the goods and, thus, the marketing of the defendant's products was contrary to fair trading practice.

1. Unfair Trade Practices Act No. 1061 of 22 December 1978 as amended by Act No. 405 of 30 May 1986 and Act No. 810 of 24 August 1990.
2. P.-L. Haarmann pp. 194*ff.*

480. Section 2 concerns misleading marketing. It prohibits the use of an untruthful or misleading statement concerning one's own trade or that of another which is likely to influence the demand or supply of a commodity or to injure the trade of another. Furthermore, it prohibits the use of any statement which is improper with regard to its contents or manner or form of representation and which is likely to injure the trade of another. The provision may be applied, for example, in cases concerning comparative marketing or in cases concerning the misleading use of statements about the kind, quality, or commercial or geographical origin of the goods.

481. A trader infringing Sections 1, 2 or 3, may be enjoined from continuing or repeating the practice. The injunction is issued by the Market Court. The Board on Business Practice of the Central Chamber of Commerce issues statements to the Market Court concerning such cases.

482. Counterfeiting. Acts Nos. 1699 and 1700 of 22 December 1995 harmonised Finnish legislation with EC Council Regulation No. 3295/94 laying down measures to prohibit the release for free circulation, export, re-export or entry for a suspensive procedure of counterfeit and pirated goods. Chapter 6a of the Trademarks Act was repealed and the relevant provisions were brought into Section 25 of the Customs Act. Section 25, paragraph 3 provides that the customs service may give information to the proprietor concerning counterfeit goods or probably counterfeit goods. The provision is to be applied alongside the Regulation referred to above.

Chapter 5. Trade Names

§1. SOURCES – LEGISLATION

Bibliography:
Castrén, M., *'Toiminimi'* [Trade Name], Finnish Lawyers' Publishing Company, Mikkeli 1984;
Castrén, M., *'Sukunimen sisältävän toiminimen suojasta'* [On the Protection of a Trade Name Containing a Surname], in LM No. 6, 1988, pp. 573–581;
Huttunen, A., *'Kaupparekisteri ja toiminimi'* [Trade Register and Trade Name], 1965;
Lehtola, J., *'Differens och förväxlingsbarhet i ljuset av handelsregister- och firmalagen'*, [Difference and Confusing Similarity in the Trade Names and Trade Register Acts], NIR 1985, pp. 528–533;
Siponen, A., *'Tavaramerkin ja toiminimen suhde'* [The Relationship between a Trade Mark and a Trade Name], in the work *'Tavaramerkki'* [Trade Mark], Helsinki 1983;
Tiili, V., *'Firmas differens och förväxlingsbarhet'* [Difference and Confusing Similarity of Trade Names], NIR 1985, pp. 534–538.

Official documents:
Government Bill 1978/238;
Government Bill 1989/210;
Committee Report KM 1969: B 102.

483. The function of trade names was acknowledged at a quite early stage in Finland: the first Trade Names Act dates back to 1895. The real breakthrough for trade names came with industrialisation. As direct contact between producers and consumers became rarer, trade names became essential for individualisation and as a means of competition. A new Trade Names Act[1] was prepared in the 1970s in order to meet the new challenges of modern business life. The reform of trade name legislation was prepared through Nordic co-operation, but only Finland and Sweden finally passed new Acts of Parliament in this field.

1. Act No. 128 of 2 February 1979. Government Bill 1978/238.

484. Finland has ratified the Paris Convention. This provides that foreign trade names are to be protected in Finland as well, without any formal registration. Accordingly, it has been argued that a trade name which is protected in another country also enjoys protection in Finland and there are no requirements pertaining to registration or establishment in Finland. However, the situation is not entirely clear on this point and it has been argued that foreign companies obtain protection in Finland under the same conditions as Finnish companies.[1]

1. M. Castrén (1984) pp. 46–48.

485. The Trade Names Act includes material provisions on trade names such as the function of a trade name, the conditions for obtaining protection, validity, transferability and sanctions for misuse. The registration procedure is governed by the *Trade Register Act*.[1]

1. Act No. 129 of 2 February 1979.

§2. THE PROTECTION OF TRADE NAMES

486. A *trade name* is the name under which a trader carries on a business (Sect. 1 of the Trade Names Act). Only traders may use a trade name. A trader is a natural or a legal person engaged in economic activity [doing economic business] on a professional basis. The concept of trader includes all kinds of undertakings and professions such as gardeners, hunters, fishermen, farmers, etc.[1]

1. The concept of a trader is defined in detail in Sect. 3 of the Trade Register Act.

487. The purpose of a trade name is to differentiate a trader. The business of a private trader can be organised as a group of entities where each entity has its own trade name. Legal persons may use just one trade name. Companies may, however, organise their businesses under *auxiliary trade names*. For example, the company as a whole may have a single trade name, whereas its various divisions have auxiliary trade names. Any trader may, in addition to a trade name, use *secondary trade names*. Secondary trade names may not be registered, but may become protected by establishment. A secondary trade name may consist, for example, of abbreviations or short versions of the trade name or of the auxiliary trade name. It may also be a figure, a sound or even the mode of dress of the employees. Trade names may be registered in various languages as *parallel trade names* (Sect. 11).[1]

1. In *SAC 1983 II 167*, the Supreme Administrative Court held that there were no obstacles to registration of a parallel trade name in Chinese letters.

488. Requirements for obtaining protection. The exclusive right to a trade name and an auxiliary trade name is obtained by registration or establishment (Sect. 2). Registration is the most common way to obtain protection. Secondary marks, however, may obtain protection only by establishment.[1] Section 2 of the Trade Register Act provides that new businesses must be entered in the Trade Register at the National Board of Patents and Registration (the Patent Office) and that the notice is to include the trade name of the business. Legal persons, certain traders and undertakings are obliged to file such a notice, which means that all companies must register their name (Sect. 3).

1. Note that secondary trade names may often be protected as trademarks.

489. The following requirements must be met in order for a trade name to be registered:

1. the applicant must be a trader,
2. the trade name must meet certain requirements with regard to its form and structure (Sect. 7 of the Trade Names Act),[1]

3. the trade name must be distinguishing (Sect. 8), it must not be liable to mislead the public and it must not be contrary to law and order, or offend public morals (Sect. 9),[2]
4. there must be no obstacles to registration (Sect. 10), and
5. the trade name must be clearly distinguishable from prior registered marks.[3]

   1. The most important requirement is that the trade name includes the company form.
   2. A trade name is misleading when it gives an incorrect impression of the company form, the products of the company, the scale of operations, etc.
   3. This requirement is based on the Trade Register Act and is of technical character.

490. In order to fulfil the purpose of individualising the business and minimising the risk of confusion among clients and business partners, the trade name must be clearly different from previously registered trade names (Sect. 8).[1] A trade name is not individualising if it characterises the business only generally. A trade name that consists of two parts that are not individualising as such, may together form an acceptable trade name. This requirement corresponds to the requirement of distinguishing power for trademarks.[2]

   1. A. Huttunen pp. 219, 225.
   2. *See* J. Lehtola pp. 529*ff.*

491. A trade name is to be registered when it meets the requirements imposed by Sections 4–6 of the Trade Names Act (Sect. 20 of the Trade Register Act). Where the trade name does not meet the requirements, the application is inadequate or there are other obstacles to registration, the Register Authority must give the applicant an opportunity to express his view on the matter or take any measures necessary (Sect. 21 of the Trade Register Act).

SC 1994:23 (Iveco v. Iweco Oy)
The Supreme Court held that the auxiliary trade name 'Iveco' of a Dutch company registered in 1975 was also reasonably wellknown among the relevant business circles in Finland before the trade name 'Iweco Oy' was registered in 1977 for a Finnish company in the same line of business. Therefore, and since the two trade names were liable to be confused, the registration of 'Iweco Oy' was cancelled.

492. Section 10 provides that certain official names, a name of another person, a title of a work protected by copyright, or a protected trademark, a secondary trade name or a trademark of another person may not be registered as trade names. All of these obstacles to registration are relative, i.e. the trade name may be registered with due permission.[1]

   1. A. Siponen p. 61, M. Castrén (1988) p. 577.

493. Protection by *establishment* is obtained when a sign or an expression is generally known by the clients and business partners of the holder of a name or mark.[1] The protection is valid only in that part of the country where the trade name is used and may be considered to be established. A secondary trade name may not be registered and protection of secondary marks may, consequently, be obtained only by establishment. The rules concerning establishment with regard to trademarks are *mutatis mutandis* applicable also to trade names.[2]

1. See e.g. *SC 1979 II 117*.
2. *See* Chapter 4.

494. Section 4 of the Trade Names Act provides that a trader may use his *own surname* as trade name, provided that this does not cause confusion with another protected trade name or trademark.[1]

1. *Court of Appeal of Helsinki* judgment of 5 July 1987: It was held that the trade names 'Oy Tillander Ab' and 'Oy A. Tillander Ab' for two jewellers were not liable to be confused.

495. Scope of protection. The exclusive right to a trade name means that other traders in Finland may not use trade names which are liable to be confused with the protected trade name (Sect. 3). 'Use' of a trademark refers to all kinds of use within the business, e.g. in letters, in advertising, etc.

496. Two trade names are liable to be confused only if they are used in the same or similar lines of business (Sect. 5). When assessing the risk of confusion between two marks, regard is paid to visual and acoustic similarity as well as to similarity of content. On rare occasions, the business value of a very well established trade name could be affected by a similar trade name used in another line of business. In such cases two trade names may be regarded as liable to be confused even though they are not used in the same line of business (the so-called Kodak doctrine and the Rat poison doctrine) (Sect. 5, para. 2).[1]

1. *See also* Chapter 4 concerning the Kodak doctrine and the Rat poison doctrine with regard to trademarks. However, note that the requirements for the Kodak doctrine to be applicable are stricter for trade names than for trademarks. *See also* V. Tiili p. 534.

497. A registered trade name enjoys protection throughout Finland, whereas an established trade name enjoys protection only in those parts of Finland in which the trade name is established.[1] However, in practice many trade names are used only in some parts of Finland. Therefore, Section 3, paragraph 1 provides that a later trade name may be used regardless of whether it is liable to be confused with a prior trade name where it is shown that the use of the later trade name does not damage the prior trade name.

1. M. Castrén (1988) pp. 573–574.

498. Where two trade names which are liable to be confused with each other are used by different traders, the one whose trade name was protected earlier has priority (Sect. 6, para. 1). However, the passivity rule applies to trade names in the same way as to trademarks. This means that where the proprietor of a prior trade name takes no measures within a reasonable time to prevent the use of another trade name, and the other trade name has become established, then the proprietor of the prior trade name forfeits his right with regard to the later trade name (Sect. 6, para. 2).

SAC 1987:13 (Finndent)
X had registered Finndent as a trademark. In the course of a co-operation agreement, X had given its consent for another company to use the trade name Finndent Oy. After the agreement terminated the registration of the trade name Finndent Oy was cancelled and the other company was prohibited from using the trade name Finndent Oy.

499. Term of protection. The registration of the trade name remains in force as long as the business exists. The protection of an established trade name expires when it ceases to be established. The authorities may, however, take action to prohibit the use of a registered trade name if it does not meet the conditions for registration (Sect. 19). A registered or established trade name may be prohibited if it has become contrary to public order or is misleading (Sect. 18). Registration may also be cancelled if, for no good cause, the trade name has not been used during the last five years.

500. Transfer. A trade name is not freely transferable. Section 13 of the Trade Names Act provides that a trade name is transferable only in connection with the transfer of the business. A business is regarded as having been transferred only where the transferee can be considered to have continued the business. If the trade name is transferred with the business and the trade name contains the name of someone other than the new owner, then a due addition is to be made to the trade name in order to clarify the situation.[1]

1. A. Huttunen pp. 258–259.

501. Infringement and remedies. The Trade Names Act provides for recourse to sanctions in cases of infringement of protected trade names. The principal sanctions are as follows: a court may impose a ban in cases where exclusivity has been infringed (Sect. 18). A penalty may further be sought when the infringement is intentional (Sect. 22). The awarding of damages implies intention or cause by the delinquent party (Sect. 23). Finally, the court may employ the precautionary measures listed in Section 24, according to which the delinquent party may be ordered to remove the protected trade name from packages, signs, etc.

Chapter 6. Industrial Design

§1. Sources – Legislation

Bibliography:
Aro, P.-L. & Kolster, L., Q73 'Report in the Name of the Finnish Group', in AIPPI Annuaire 1982/I, p. 118;
Haarmann, P.-L., *'Immateriaalioikeuden oppikirja'* [A Textbook of Intellectual Property Rights] 2nd ed., Finnish Lawyers' Publishing Company, Helsinki 1994;
Koktvedgaard, M. & Levin, M., *'Lärobok i immaterialrätt'* [A Textbook of Intellectual Property Rights], Nordstedts Juridik, Stockholm 1995;
Levin, M., *'Formskydd'* [Design Protection], Liberförlag, Stockholm 1984;
Tiili, V., *'Skydd för varuutstyrsel enligt mönsterrättslagen, varumärkeslagen och konkurrensrätten'* [Design Protection in Registered Design, Trade Mark and Competition Law], in NIR No. 2, 1983, pp. 173–198;
Tiili, V. & Aro, P.-L., *'Yrityksen tavaramerkki- ja mallisuojaopas'* [An Enterprise's Guide to Trade Marks and Design Protection] 1st ed., Kauppalehti Business Books, Jyväskylä 1986.

Official documents and publications:
Government Bill 1970/113;
Committee Report 1966: A 13.

502. The Registered Designs Act[1] entered into force in 1971 following Nordic joint preparation. Prior to 1971 there was no separate legislation in Finland on the protection of industrial designs. It was in this year that the other Nordic countries enacted new legislation on the protection of industrial designs. Before 1971, however, the owner of an industrial design in certain cases enjoyed a limited protection through the Copyright Act and the Unfair Competition Act.

1. Act No. 221 of 12 March 1971.

503. Industrial design is internationally protected by the Paris Convention. As the provisions of the Paris Convention are relatively brief, international harmonisation is undeveloped and the protection of industrial designs varies from country to country.

504. Nordic legislation on industrial designs is based on the so-called patent approach, in contrast to certain other countries where it is based on the copyright approach. It has been claimed that the Nordic solution has not been entirely successful, as a more general protection would be more appropriate than the formal registration procedure and requirement of originality under patent law.[1]

1. M. Koktvedgaard & M. Levin p. 264.

505. In 1996 there were 864 applications to register an industrial design, 458 of which were foreign. The average time taken for processing applications was nine months.

§2. Subject Matter of Protection

506. The Registered Designs Act protects 'the prototype of an article's appearance or of an ornament' (Sect. 1). The term 'article' refers to a concrete object which has been produced industrially or by a craftsman. Protection is not granted to interior design, landscape architecture, hair styling, etc. The size of the article is of no importance. Under ordinary circumstances only the entire article may be granted design protection, but if a particular part of the article may be sold separately from the rest of the article, e.g. a spare part, then that particular part may also be granted design protection.

507. It is the visual appearance which is protected. This means that whatever is not part of the visual appearance is not protected, e.g. constructions displayed as technical drawings. As it is the prototype of the appearance which enjoys protection, the article itself need not actually exist. An ornament may also receive protection. By an ornament is generally understood a two-dimensional design for a decoration. Examples of ornaments include the designs of curtains, porcelain and carpets. It has also been claimed that the tread of a tyre is one kind of three-dimensional design.[1]

> 1. Haarmann, on the other hand, has claimed that the tread of a tyre cannot be protected as an ornament, P.-L. Haarmann p. 137.

508. Design protection exclusively protects the particular pattern represented by the design. Simple technical or functional solutions are not protected by the Registered Designs Act. However, a pattern may indirectly be granted limited protection, which means that design protection is actively utilised by certain industrial sectors.

§3. Conditions for Protection

509. Three requirements must be satisfied in order for a design to enjoy the right of registration. The conditions are that the design is (1) the result of creative work, (2) original and (3) substantially different from previous designs.

510. The requirement of creativity. Section 1, paragraph 2 states that the 'creator' of a design may acquire exclusive rights thereto. This implies that the design must have been created by a natural person, i.e. that the design of natural phenomenon such as flowers, stones or tree stumps cannot acquire protection. Representations of these phenomena may, however, acquire protection. That a design must be the result of a creative intellectual effort means that a design which is an imitation is not granted protection.[1] This also means that so-called commonplace designs are not granted protection. Examples of commonplace designs are various kinds of ordinary stripes, squares, balls, etc.

1. Committee Report 1966: A 13 p. 19.

511. The requirement of originality. According to Section 2, a design may only be registered if it substantially differs from what was known before the date of application for registration. The requirement of originality is similar to the originality requirement in the Patents Act.[1] Anything which has been made available to the public, including previous applications for patents, trademarks and utility models, are not considered to be original. The requirement of originality is absolute and objective in the same way as in the Patents Act. Anything that has been made available to the public as the result of a reproduction, exhibition or offer for sale may not be registered as an original design. However, a design may be registered even though it has become available to the public, during a period of six months prior to the application, where such publication occurred through manifest abuse or at an officially recognised international exhibition.

1. P.-L. Haarmann p. 138.

512. As with the Patents Act (*cf.* Chapter 2, §3), the holder of a right may be protected by Convention priority (Sect. 8). The priority period is six months counted from the date of the first application (*see* Registered Designs Decree Sects. 8–11).

513. The requirement of substantial difference. Section 2 provides that the design must substantially differ from what was previously known. This notion of degree of *difference* corresponds to the idea of *inventive step* used in the Patents Act. When assessing the degree of difference in design, the overall impression is decisive, i.e. difference means more than minor variations of detail. Requirements of originality and difference have been less restrictive in product design applications where the degree of possible variation in the type of product is slight. In uncertain cases decisions concerning the requirement of substantial difference may be based on the judgment of professionals within the branch in question. This means that the degree of similarity is not decided on the basis of, for example, whether consumers judge the goods to be similar.[1]

1. V. Tiili pp. 181*ff.* Compare with the trademark legislation.

514. The requirement of substantial difference is generally interpreted strictly. This is particularly so in the textile, clothing and furniture industries. Otherwise damaging barriers to competition could arise.[1] It has been claimed that the requirement of substantial difference has not received sufficient attention in registration applications. The result is that in Finland the protection of industrial design has not provided effective protection.[2]

1. M. Koktvedgaard & M. Levin p. 278.
2. V. Tiili pp. 182*ff.*, P.-L. Aro & L. Kolster p. 118.

515. Impediments to registration. Although a design meets the requirements of creativity, originality and substantial difference, it may not be registered if there are other impediments to registration. The impediments to registration are listed in Section 4. The first impediment to registration arises if the design *conflicts with morality or public order.* This is the only absolute impediment to registration.[1] In practice the provision is of limited importance. The remaining limitations are that the design may not be registered without permission if it includes:

1. a national flag, coat of arms, emblem, mark or stamp of inspection, abbreviation or anything similar thereto;
2. anything which may be understood to be another person's trade name, trade symbol, trademark, surname, artistic name, portrait, etc.;
3. anything that may be interpreted as the title of another person's protected literary or artistic work or infringes their copyright or right to a photographic image;
4. anything that does not differ substantially from a design registered in Finland in the name of another person; or
5. anything that does not differ substantially from a utility model registered in Finland in the name of another person.

1. The others are relative.

§4. Formalities (Procedure for Granting and Acquiring Protection)

516. The formal provisions on registration are covered in Sections 9–23. An application for registration is to be addressed to the National Board of Patents and Registration. The registration procedure is similar to the registration of a patent. The main difference lies in the examination of originality which is less extensive. The applicant must affirm that to the best of his knowledge the design is not readily available to the public.

517. In practice the examination of originality by the National Board of Patents and Registration is limited to designs which have been registered in Finland and to applications which are pending at the time of application.

518. The application must specify the items and categories of items for which registration is being sought. A single application may include a maximum of twenty designs excluding ornaments (*multiple registration*) (Sect. 11). A condition for this is that the items for which the design is sought are related in respect of manufacture and use, for example a dinner service, porcelain, clothes, furniture, various spare parts, etc. Designs with certain common features may also be registered, provided that the application is filed on the same day and that the designs do not substantially differ from one another (Registered Designs Decree, Sect. 22).

Industrial Design, Ch. 6

§5. Ownership and Transfer (Assignment – Licences)

519. The right to a design belongs to the person named in the application who has created the design. The creator of a design may assign the right thereto. There are no separate provisions governing the assignment of a design right within an employment relationship. In general, the right should pass directly to the employer unless otherwise agreed. In cases of especially valuable designs, it is assumed that copyright protection exists, meaning that the principles of copyright law apply to the transfer of rights to such designs.[1]

    1. M. Koktvedgaard & M. Levin p. 281.

520. A design right may be transferred under such circumstances as inheritance, donation, division of estate and bankruptcy. A design right is a property right subject to the general rules on transfer and licencing. However, the licencing of design rights is to some degree limited by the law of copyright. A licensee may not assign his right without the consent of the holder of the design right. However, this does not apply to the transfer of a business (Sect. 26).[1]

    1. M. Koktvedgaard & M. Levin p. 280.

521. The transfer of a design right or of a licence, as well as a lien on a design right, may be registered in the design register. Registration is not mandatory, but in the event of litigation the holder of the design right is considered to be the person who is registered as such. Registration is important in cases where the owner of the design has transferred the right to another person as well as in cases of foreclosure and bankruptcy (Sects. 26–27).

§6. Scope of Exclusive Rights

522. A design right gives the exclusive right to use the design in the course of trade. The owner of the right enjoys the exclusive right to exploit the design by making, importing, marketing, offering for sale, assigning or hiring out an article which *does not substantially differ* from the design, or which includes something which does not substantially differ from it. The right to the design only includes articles or similar articles for which the design has been registered. As the provisions are exhaustive, it is permissible, for example, to depict a design protected article.[1] The design may be registered in one or more categories of classification of articles. In theory, the administrative classification of articles is of no importance in determining the scope of the protection of the design. In practice, however, the administrative categories of classification are helpful in decisions concerning the scope of protection.[2]

    1. Provided that it is not already protected.
    2. M. Koktvedgaard & M. Levin p. 283.

523. The Registered Designs Act primarily covers *economic rights*. However, the application for the registration of a design must specify who has created the design (Sect. 10, para. 2).

§7. Limitations on the Scope of Protection

524. Exhaustion. In the same way as the Patent Act, the Registered Designs Act is territorially limited to the area of the European Union (community exhaustion). This means that the possessor of the right cannot use the right to prevent the use of articles within the European Economic Area. In other words, design protected articles may be freely exported and imported within the EEA. Protected articles may not, however, be imported into the European Economic Area without the permission of the possessor of the right and articles which have been placed in circulation with his permission may not be circulated elsewhere.

525. Private use. As has been mentioned above, design rights are limited to the course of trade. Protection does not therefore extend to private use.

526. Prior right of use. Any person who, in the course of trade, has been using the design when an application for registration of the said design is filed may, without hindrance, continue to make use of the design. Such a right may only be transferred in connection with the transfer of a business.

527. Aircraft, etc. The protected spare parts and fittings for an aircraft may be imported and used for aircraft of foreign origin.

528. Compulsory licence. In a manner similar to the Patent Act, a compulsory licence may be granted to a person who was using the design when the registration application became public (Sects. 28–30). This is a variety of the extended right of use which is of no practical importance.

§8. Duration of Protection

529. The registration of a design is valid for *five years*, from the date of application for registration. Registration may be renewed for two additional five year periods. The maximum period of protection is therefore fifteen years reckoned from the date of application. An application for renewal must be filed at the National Board of Patents and Registration no sooner than one year before, and no later than six months before the period of registration expires.

530. A registration may be cancelled, transferred or deleted from the register in a manner similar to that provided for in the Patents Act (Sects. 31–33). A registration must be cancelled when the registration of the design is in conflict with any of the requirements listed in Sections 1–4 and an impediment to registration continues to exist. The cancellation of a registration most often occurs in cases of infringement.

§9. Infringement and Remedies

531. In cases of alleged infringement, the registered design is compared with the article constituting an alleged infringement. The extent of design protection depends on the concrete content of the registration documents, i.e. the quality, clarity and classification of the protected article are of prime importance. A decision as to whether an infringement has occurred depends on whether the article constituting an alleged infringement clearly differs from the registered design. The scope of protection is the same as the scope of difference at the time of registration. In decisions concerning the scope of protection the date of registration is decisive.[1]

1. M. Koktvedgaard & M. Levin pp. 283–284.

532. Sections 35–44 contain provisions on legal proceedings, sanctions and the consequences of an infringement of a design right. These are similar to the sanctions and consequences arising in the case of an infringement of a patent right.[1]

1. *See* Chapter 2.

§10. Overlapping and Relation to Other Intellectual Property Laws

533. As has already been stated, the same article may be protected both by design registration and by copyright. In such instances, copyright and design right do not limit one another. In certain instances it is possible that an item with a protected design may also be protected as a trademark. In such instances the design right and the right to a trademark similarly do not limit one another.

Chapter 7. Plant Variety Protection

§1. SOURCES – LEGISLATION

Bibliography:
Aro, P.-L., *'Kasvinjalostajan oikeudellisesta asemasta – kehityskulkuja ja näkymiä'* [The Legal Status of the Plant Breeder – Trends and Perspectives], Vammala 1977;
'Bioteknologiska uppfinningar och immaterialrätten i Norden' [Biotechnological Inventions and Intellectual Property Law in the Nordic Countries], Nordiska Ministerrådet, I NORD 1988:99, II NORD 1992:8;
Crespi, R.S., 'Patents and Plant Variety Rights: Is There an Interface Problem?', International Review of Industrial Property and Copyright Law, Vol. 23 No. 2, 1992, pp. 168–184;
Greengrass, B., 'The 1991 Act on the UPOV Convention', European Intellectual Property Review 1991, pp. 466–472;
Moufang, R., 'Protection for Plant Breeding and Plant Varieties', NIR 3/1992;
Straus, J., 'Biotechnologische Erfindungen – ihr Schutz und seine Grenzen', GRUR 1992/4, pp. 252–266;
Vuori, A., *'Elävän materiaalin oikeussuojan laajuudesta – kysymyksiä oikeudesta ja kohtuudesta'* [On the Scope of Legal Protection for Living Material – Questions of Rights and Reasonableness], LM 2/1993, pp. 195–217.

Official documents and publications:
Kasvinjalostajantoimikunnan mietintö [Report of the Plant Breeder Committee], KM 1990:36.

534. The need for legal protection granted to the breeder of an improved plant variety for the said plant was recognised in Finland in the 1970s. An Act of Parliament was passed in 1977 on the encouragement of improved plant varieties which primarily regulated economic subsidies for improved plant varieties in Finland. The Act imposed an improved plant variety government levy on trade in seeds for tilled land and green open space plants. The proceeds from the fee were channelled to the breeders of improved plant varieties in the form of an improved plant variety subsidy. The Act was described as a public improved plant variety law. In addition to the payment of an improved plant variety fee, the breeder of such a plant variety could also pay a so-called innovation charge for innovative varieties as long as the variety was not commonly grown.

535. The 1980s has witnessed a significant increase in interest in improved plant varieties in the industrialised countries. The main reason is that the rights of the breeders of improved plant varieties have been recognised in the legislation of many countries. The protection of plant varieties has above all increased the interest of private firms in plant varieties. Countries which do not recognise the rights of the breeders of improved plant varieties have difficulty in getting protected varieties for cultivation. Finland recognised the need for stronger protection of breeders

Plant Variety Protection, Ch. 7

and, in 1988, a working group at the Ministry of Agriculture and Forestry proposed that a new law on the rights of breeders of improved plant varieties be drafted. Similarly to the other Nordic countries and European states, the patent law of Finland forbids the patenting of plant varieties in Finland.[1]

1. Patents Act (No. 550 of 1967), Sect. 1 para 4. The legislation concerning biotechnical inventions has been developed within the EU and the European Patent Convention (EPC). *See* Chapter 2.

536. A new Plant Variety Protection Act (No. 789 of 1992) entered into force in 1992.[1] The content of the Act corresponds to the provisions of the International Convention for the Protection of New Varieties of Plants (UPOV). The major aim is to secure the financing of work on the improvement of plant varieties and the use of innovative varieties. With the entry into force of the new Act, Finland met the requirements of the UPOV Convention and ratified the 1978 Convention in 1994.

1. Government Bill No. 24 of 1992, amended by Government Bill No. 94 of 1993.

537. The International Convention for the Protection of New Varieties of Plants (Union pour la Protection des Obtentions Végétales of 1961, revised in 1978 and 1991)[1] has been ratified by a majority of the OECD countries, including all the Nordic countries. The organisation which the member countries have created supervises compliance with the convention principles and further develops them. According to the UPOV Convention, plant breeding law means that breeders of plants are granted the exclusive right to the commercial exploitation of the propagating material which they have improved. According to the Convention, the Member States are to apply the principle of national treatment,[2] i.e. the breeder in another Member State is to enjoy the same rights that the country in question grants to its own breeders. The 1978 Convention is based on so-called double protection, i.e. a patent cannot be granted to varieties which have been granted a plant breeder right. This double protection has been discarded in the 1991 Convention.[3] In the UPOV Convention, the minimum period of protection is fifteen years and for garden plants with a trunk this period is eighteen years.

1. The UPOV Convention of 1991 has not yet entered into force as five states have not ratified the revised convention.
2. P.-L. Aro p. 28.
3. Finnish law is still based on double protection. The discarding of double protection and membership of the 1991 UPOV Convention is under discussion. *See also* J. Straus p. 265.

538. In 1994 the Council of the European Union enacted a Decree on the right of plant breeders.[1] The Decree created a Community Plant Variety Authority which, in addition to the legislation of the Member States on the right of plant breeders, can grant rights which are in force across the entire Community. National legislation is not harmonised but is applicable in parallel to the regulation of the Community. The Decree contains the recognised principles of distinguishability, uniformity and permanence as well as the requirement of novelty and the type of name for a plant breeder right to be granted. In contrast to Finnish plant breeder rights, Community plant breeder rights can be granted jointly to several people. The consumer principle is applied in a similar manner as in the case of other industrial rights (Art. 16). Under the Decree, the exclusive right to protected plants is limited so as to protect agricultural products and the public interest through so-called forced cultivation. Protection can be granted for 25 to 30 years, depending on the kind of plant. In the application of the Decree, the UPOV Convention, TRIPS and the EPC Convention are observed.[2]

1. Council Decree No. 2100 of 1994 on the Rights of Plant Breeders in the Community, *OJ* 1 September 1994 L 227.
2. A proposed directive on patenting biotechnical inventions has also been submitted but has not yet been accepted by the European Parliament, COM(88) 496 final.

539. Article 27 of the TRIPS Agreement concerns patents. According to this article, inventions which satisfy the customary patent requirements are granted an exclusive right. This article also covers all kinds of plants. However, Article 27 gives countries the right to exempt plants which have been improved in a traditional way from patent protection on the condition that the plant type is effectively protected in another way.

§2. SUBJECT MATTER OF PROTECTION

540. The aim of the 1992 Plant Variety Protection Act was to create the conditions for the financing of plant breeding and to secure access to appropriate foreign types of plants for cultivation in Finland. Plant breeding attempts to improve the traits of cultivated plants in order to maximise and guarantee their harvest, which in turn is important for profitability. The traits that are developed above all are resistance to disease and the ability of the plant to make effective use of nutritive matter. The climate in Finland imposes special demands on the kinds of plants that are cultivated and it is therefore important that the domestic plant breeding industry is maintained and developed.

541. The rights of plant breeders mean that the person who has, in a decisive manner, bred a new kind of plant can register this breed and thereby obtain an exclusive right to its commercial exploitation for a limited time (Sect. 1). The term 'plant breeder' refers to a physical person, in contrast to the UPOV Convention which applies to both natural and legal persons. If a plant is bred by a person employed by another person, then the question of title to exclusive rights is resolved according to the employment relationship, i.e. if the plant type has been bred by the employee of a breeding institution, then the institution (employer) is considered to hold title to the right.

542. The idea of a variety is understood as a variety of breed of plant, in botanical terms a variety is a group of individual plants distinguishable on the basis of its morphological, physiological, chemical or other traits. Breeders' rights are granted both to varieties arising directly from breeding and to varieties which have not required breeding, provided that the requirements of Section 4 concerning distinctiveness, homogeneous stability and uniformity have been met.[1]

Plant Variety Protection, Ch. 7

1. B. Greengrass p. 467, R. Crespi pp. 170*ff.*, and Bioteknologiska uppfinningar och immaterialrätten i Norden I 1988:99 pp. 4*ff.*

543. Breeder rights can be granted to all plant genera and species the cultivation or importation of which has commercial value in Finland (Sect. 2). The Decree on Plant Genera and Species (No. 905 of 1992) sets further conditions on the kind of breeder right that can be granted. In the first place, breeder rights are granted to plants bred in Finland including plants cultivated in Finland which have not been bred there, in order to secure the supply of foreign kinds of material. In 1992 the number of types of plants protected by breeders' rights was 160.

§3. Conditions of Protection

544. The granting of breeders rights is conditional upon the variety being of commercial importance (Sect. 2). An additional requirement is that the variety must be homogeneous and sufficiently stable to have recognisable traits (Sect. 4). Breeder rights can only be granted to a new variety of plant which, through at least one significant trait, can be distinguished from earlier known varieties. The idea of distinguishability refers to the fact that the traits can be defined morphologically, physiologically or chemically. Breeder rights can be granted to a new variety which distinguishes itself from earlier known varieties by, for example, its colour; such as a black tulip. When the possibility of distinguishing a new variety is investigated, the type is compared with earlier known varieties.

545. Breeder rights, as with other industrial rights, require that the variety must be new in relation to what was known before the day on which the application was filed. The application for a breeder right makes the variety known only if the breeder right is granted. According to Section 5, a variety may not be registered if the cultivation material of the variety has been offered for sale or marketed in Finland with the consent of its owner before the application was filed. The marketing of the variety for some time outside Finland before the application is filed is no impediment to registration: cultivation material for grapes and certain trees may have been marketed abroad for no more than six years and, in the case of other plants for no more than four years. The reason for permitting a certain amount of marketing is to give foreign breeders an opportunity to assess whether there is a demand for their varieties.

§4. Formalities (Procedure for Granting and Acquiring Protection)

546. The exclusive right to a variety of plant, a breeder right, is acquired through registration. Applications for registration are filed at the Plant Variety Board[1] which is subordinate to the Ministry of Agriculture and Forestry and serves as the registration authority under the Plant Variety Protection Act (Sect. 9). Applications for registration must be submitted in writing and, in addition to information about the applicant, contain a description of how the new variety differs from other varieties, the name of the variety and an assurance given by the applicant pursuant to Section 5 that the variety has not been in circulation. As it is not, in practice, possible for the authority to supervise whether the variety has been in circulation according to Section 5, a system of assurances given by the applicant has been used.[2] The completed application is given a preliminary examination and is made public if there are no formal obstacles to registration.

1. The Board has expertise in biology, plant classification and law.
2. A penalty for providing false information and registration offences is prescribed in the Penal Code.

547. For a variety to be distinguishable from other varieties, the variety name is important. Section 11 gives the criteria for registering a variety name. The variety name is a genetic description, by contrast with a trademark which is a name. A registered variety name is used for the protected plant material independently of the producer. Its purpose is to identify the variety material, and not the producer as in the case of trademarks. Ideally the variety name should be short and descriptive, but it may not be a name referring to a certain general trait. It is also recommended that the variety name should be suitable for international use without being translated.

548. The name of the variety must not be likely to mislead the public, i.e. to give a false picture of the traits, origin, value or breeder of the variety. The name of the variety must not be contrary to law, public order or morals. A variety name which can be confused with some other variety name or protected trademark, or which only consists of numbers cannot be accepted. The registering authorities in the Member States of the UPOV organisation can oppose the registration of a variety name in another Member State, as the application is sent to these authorities for information purposes.

549. According to Section 12, variety owners who have filed a registration application in another UPOV state are granted priority if, within twelve months of the application, they request plant breeder rights in Finland, i.e. the application is deemed to have been filed in Finland on the same day as the earlier application. Priority is granted only if it is expressly requested in the application within the prescribed time limit.

550. If an application is incomplete, then within a prescribed time limit the applicant has the right to complete the application or to submit a statement in the case of any obstacle to registration that may arise. Only after the applicant has submitted such a statement may the registering authority reject the application if obstacles to registration still remain (Sects. 13–14).

551. Claims to stronger rights are treated in the Plant Variety Protection Act in a manner similar to cases involving other industrial rights (Sect. 16). The provisions on public announcement in Section 17 give the public an opportunity to file counterclaims against pending applications. The purpose of this section is to allow the settlement of disputed ownership rights already at the application stage.

Plant Variety Protection, Ch. 7

552. The registering authority may settle disputed ownership rights only in clear cases or in those which are based on an agreement between the parties. In other cases a court must decide on the merits of the various claims. A claim to a stronger right may be submitted at any time during the processing of the application before the variety is registered. If a counterclaim is successful, then the original application is transferred to the person who has demonstrated a stronger right to the variety, and the applicant need not file a new application (Sect. 17). Cases in which two breeders have independently bred varieties of the same kind which might be confused with each other are not a matter of stronger right. The exclusive breeder right is then granted to the person whose application was filed first (priority in time).

553. According to Section 18, the actual examination takes place when the registering authority, assisted by the applicant, examines whether the variety satisfies the requirements set out in Section 4 (distinguishability, homogeneous stability and constancy). The decision on registration may be made no sooner than after the period for claims has elapsed. The time from the filing of an application to registration is usually some two to three years because of the cultivation period.

554. Registration of the name of the variety takes place at the same time as protection of the right to the variety (Sect. 20). Both registration and the rejection of an application must be made public.

§5. Ownership and Transfer (Assignment – Licences)

555. The owner of the exclusive right to a registered plant variety is, in the first instance, the person who has bred the variety (Sect. 1). According to Section 3, the right to the plant breed may be granted to breeders who have bred the variety in Finland or to those to whom the right has been transferred. According to the UPOV Convention, the Member States of the organisation are to honour the principle of national acceptance, which means that breeders who are citizens of a UPOV state (or their assignees) are also to be granted breeder rights in Finland. The Ministry of Agriculture and Forestry also has the authority to grant an exclusive right on other grounds if this is justifiable in terms of cultivation or importation to Finland.

556. The owners of plant varieties may, through licencing, grant permission to others to commercially exploit the varieties to which they have exclusive rights based on their breeder rights. Licensees are not free to transfer their rights without the permission of the variety owner (Sect. 23). In the case of the transfer of ownership of a company, unless otherwise agreed, licences, together with their associated rights and responsibilities, are also transferred to the new owner. The transfer of and licence to the exclusive right to a registered plant variety is to be recorded in the plant variety register maintained by the registering authority. The owner of the plant variety is deemed to be the one most recently registered as the plant variety owner in the register (Sect. 23). Those to whom the owner of a plant variety has transferred the right to that variety may ascertain any possible transfer of licences free of charge by requesting information from the registering authority. The plant variety register has official standing, which is to say that the registered right applies to third parties. Anyone whatsoever has the right to obtain information from the register on payment of a fee.

557. If the reproductive material of a registered plant variety is not placed on the market under reasonable conditions and to a sufficient extent in terms of the need for food, a court may grant a compulsory licence. The compulsory licence includes the right to the reproductive material of the registered plant variety (Sect. 24). To prevent the misuse of the registered plant variety, the licence holder must have the prerequisites for exploiting the plant variety in question in an acceptable manner and under the conditions set by the court. Compulsory licences do not prevent the owner of the plant variety from exercising their rights or from granting licences to their varieties.

§6. Scope of Exclusive Rights

558. The exclusive right of the breeder means the right to use the registered variety for commercial purposes. Persons other than the owner of the plant variety may only use the variety in question with the consent of the owner. By use is meant the production or importing of the material of the variety for use as research material or for sale, or for the marketing of the reproductive material. In order to permit the owner of the plant variety to oversee the commercial exploitation of the variety in Finland, the law also states that the commercial importation of protected propagating material is governed by the Plant Variety Protection Act. The owners of plant varieties may not use their exclusive rights in Finland to act against a grower abroad who is growing varieties protected through registration in Finland.

559. The exclusive right is not only limited to food plants but also includes ornamental plants (Sect. 7) to the extent to which they are used commercially as ornamental plants or as cut flowers.

560. The exclusive right to the reproductive material of ornamental plants does not grant the grower sufficient protection as ornamental plants may be reproduced through vegetative propagation. For this reason, the scope of Section 7 also extends to the seedlings of ornamental plants and to parts which can be used for research purposes.

§7. Limitations on the Scope of Protection

561. The Plant Variety Protection Act recognises two exceptions to the exclusive right referred to above. Regardless of the exclusive right to a particular plant variety, growers always have the right to use the seeds of protected plant varieties on their own farmlands (Sect. 6: farmer's privilege).[1] The exclusive right does not extend to reproductive material produced and sold for consumption, for example grain. The Plant Variety Protection Act does not cover reproductive material sold for the purpose of consumption, even where the buyer uses the material for research.

1. A. Vuori p. 197, B. Greengrass p. 469.

562. The right to use a protected plant variety for the development of new varieties constitutes the other exception to the exclusive right (Sect. 8: breeder's exemption). This exemption is based on the recognition that the development of new varieties is traditionally based on the use of existing material. Breeder's exemption does not include the production of a variety of material if this variety is one which is produced through the substantial use of a protected variety, i.e. in cases where the variety cannot be clearly distinguished from a protected variety or where the growing material of the protected variety is used in a substantial manner in the commercial production of another variety.[1]

1. A. Vuori p. 197, Bioteknologiska uppfinningar och immaterialrätten i Norden II 1992:8 p. 37.

563. The right of the grower to exploit the breeder's exemption is conditional. It is relatively simple to develop a new variety from a protected variety which would satisfy the requirement of difference and consequently would have a right to registration. The importance of such an essentially derived variety is, however, based to a significant degree on the original variety. For this reason Section 8 requires that the owner of a protected variety must consent to the commercial exploitation of an essentially derived variety. According to the same section, the consent of the owner of the variety is also required where it is necessary to make repeated use of the protected variety in order to produce commercially another variety such as a hybrid.

§8. Duration of Protection

564. The exclusive right to a plant variety applies from the day the registration decision is made by the registering authority. Provided that the annual fee is paid within the prescribed period, the exclusive right is valid for a period of 20 years counted from the beginning of the year following the year in which the registration decision was made (Sect. 21).

565. The registered name is also to be used after the period of protection has expired or if the right has otherwise expired (Sect. 22).

566. In certain cases, the exclusive right to a variety of plant may cease even though the period of protection has not expired. The owner of a variety may renounce his right by notifying the registering authority in writing (Sect. 26). The agreement of the owner of the licence is not required for a variety to be removed from the variety register. The owner of the licence may, however, bring civil proceedings against the owner of the variety seeking damages if the voluntary loss of rights of the owner of the variety infringes the conditions set out in the licence. The right of the owner of the variety also lapses if the annual fee is not paid within the prescribed period.

567. Even if the registering authority has carefully checked that the conditions for registering the right to a plant variety have been satisfied before the variety is registered, it may subsequently turn out that one of the conditions for registering the said right has not been satisfied. In such cases, the exclusive right may be declared null and void by a court of law (Sect. 27). The registering authority may also declare the breeder's right to forfeit if the owner of the variety does not submit reproductive material of the variety with the characteristics defined when the protection was granted, or if the owner of the variety fails to comply with the request of the registering authority to provide reproductive material of the kind necessary for ascertaining that the variety is appropriately maintained (Sect. 28). A forfeiture decision made by the registering authority may be appealed to the Supreme Administrative Court (Sect. 37).

§9. INFRINGEMENT AND REMEDIES

568. The Plant Variety Protection Act includes provisions on the protection of exclusive rights which are similar to those in the Patents Act and the Trademarks Act. The court may issue an order to cease and desist from an action which violates the exclusive right to a plant variety (Sect. 29). The order to cease and desist may be made regardless of whether the action has been done in good faith or out of negligence. If the holder of the exclusive right to a plant variety considers that some action infringes upon his exclusive right, then he may bring an action to court seeking a declaratory judgment. Furthermore, a person other than the holder of the exclusive right may instigate a declaratory action if he thinks that the exclusive right to a plant variety constitutes an impediment to a particular activity (Sect. 30)

569. According to the same principles as in the Patents Act, the holder of an exclusive right to a plant variety may bring a civil action for damages where his exclusive right has been deliberately or negligently infringed. In decisions in cases involving negligence, the assumption is that enterprises operating in the field are aware of what kinds of plant variety are protected, i.e. responsibility is given a strict interpretation. The damages payable may amount to the full amount of actual damage suffered as well as compensation for any other loss incurred as a result of the infringement. The statute of limitations on claims for damages is five years counted from the date of infringement.

570. In cases involving the infringement of an exclusive right to a plant variety, the court may also order that the variety of plant material be transferred to the damaged party or that it be confiscated. However, this does not apply if the person who is in possession of the plant material has received it in good faith.

571. The court may, in certain cases, grant interim protection to a plant variety against its professional use subsequent to the filing of an application for an exclusive right but prior to the granting thereof (Sect. 33).

572. The Plant Variety Protection Act contains certain penal provisions. Wilful infringement of the exclusive right to a plant variety is punishable by a fine or by imprisonment for a period not exceeding six months (Sect. 34). The public prosecutor may not bring charges for an offence unless the injured party has reported the offence for prosecution. The Plant Variety Protection Act contains no provisions on the exclusive right to use the name of a plant variety. However, a registered plant variety name, or a name that may easily be confused with such a name, may not be used for a variety if the name of the variety is registered. The deliberate or negligent infringement of the right to the name of a plant variety is subject to a fine (Sect. 35).

§10. OVERLAPPING AND RELATION TO OTHER INTELLECTUAL PROPERTY LAWS

573. The Finnish Patent Act prohibits the patenting of plant varieties.[1] However, the National Board of Patents and Registration of Finland has interpreted the Patents Act (No. 560 of 1967) in such a way that a patent may be granted to plants and to parts of plants such as cells, which have been produced through artificial genetic means.

1. On the relationship between patents and the protection of plant breeders, see R. Moufang pp. 330–348.

Chapter 8. Chip Protection

§1. Sources – Legislation

Bibliography:
Wager, H. (ed.), *'Integroitujen piirien suojaaminen'* [Protection of Integrated Circuits], in *'Patenttioikeuden erityiskysymyksiä'* [Special Problems in Patent Law], 1988, pp. 93–144.

Official documents and publications:
Government Bill No. 161 of 1990;
Act on the Exclusive Right to the Layout-Design of an Integrated Circuit, No. 32 of 1991.

574. Creative work has traditionally been protected by the law of copyright. However, advanced technological development has resulted in a need for special protection for creative work done within the field of computer technology. The creation of integrated circuits has been of considerable importance to this development. The aim of establishing a new intellectual property right, *the exclusive right to the layout-design of an integrated circuit*, has been to encourage continuous investment in research and in the development of integrated circuits. Integrated circuits are an essential element of nearly all electronics, either in the form of microprocessors or as memory circuits for storage of information. It goes without saying that electronics is a cornerstone of many branches of industry and is also of great importance in modern private households.

575. The development and production of integrated circuits requires large investments, not least of economic resources. Development aims at miniaturisation, large capacity and profitability. The cost of making a copy of a circuit is only a fraction of its total production costs. Besides encouraging continuous investment in research and development, the law on the exclusive right to the layout-design of an integrated circuit also attempts to ensure that such circuits are used and distributed in an acceptable manner.

576. On the basis of international development and the needs of domestic industry, a law on the exclusive right to the layout-design of an integrated circuit was enacted in 1991 (Act on the Exclusive Right to the Layout-Design of an Integrated Circuit, No. 32/1991).[1] This law clarified the legal rules on integrated circuits. The copying, importing and distribution to the public of protected layout-designs for integrated circuits requires the consent of the person holding the exclusive right. The drafting of the Finnish Act took note of corresponding legislation in other countries, of Directive No. 87/54/EEC and of the WIPO Convention on the protection of integrated circuits. The level of protection in the Finnish Act is in part higher than that required by the Washington Convention of the WIPO.

1. Government Bill No. 161 of 1990.

577. The USA and Japan enacted legislation on the protection of semiconductors as long ago as in the mid-1980s and the exclusive right to the layout-design of an integrated circuit was recognised as a new intellectual property right. In 1991 the World Intellectual Property Organisation (WIPO) in Washington approved a convention on the protection of integrated circuits. The convention has still not been ratified by a sufficiently large number of states for it to enter into force. One obstacle is that the USA and Japan consider the level of protection afforded by the convention to be inadequate. International protection is maintained for the time being by agreements. In 1987 the Member States of the European Community approved a Directive (87/54/EEC) on the legal protection of the topography of semiconductors.

§2. Subject Matter of Protection

578. The Finnish Act on the protection of the layout-design of an integrated circuit protects the intellectual result of intellectually creative work, i.e. the layout-design of an integrated circuit. Section 1 of the Act defines layout-design as the three-dimensional placing of the parts of an integrated circuit in all of its possible patterns. The parts of an integrated circuit are placed or grouped so that the result is a fast and effective circuit. In technical terms, an integrated circuit comprises active and passive interconnections placed on a semiconductor substrate to form a functional entity, e.g. a transistor. A semiconductor is a material which is something between a conductor and an insulator, e.g. silicon. Circuits constructed on some substrate other than a semiconductor are not protected. For the purposes of the Act, an integrated circuit is an electric circuit in which the elements, at least one of which must be active, together with all or part of the connections between them, are housed on a semiconductor base as a functional entity, where the said circuit is intended to perform electric circuitry functions. An exclusive right may also be granted in respect of an integrated circuit which was first distributed to the public in Finland.

§3. Conditions of Protection

579. In order to receive protection, a layout-design or part thereof must be original (Sect. 2). The layout-design must consequently be the product of an independent and creative intellectual act. Layout-designs which are directly copied from another layout-design are not covered by the protection as the matter concerns the same layout-design as that of the prototype.[1] The requirement of originality does not include any real requirement of originality as in the Patents Act;[2] at the time of classification attention is given to whether, at the time of its creation, the layout-design was substantially different from registered layout-designs. If two persons have independently created the same layout-design, then both of them have the right to register the layout-design and thereby acquire an exclusive right. A layout-design that was original at the time of its creation still meets the requirements of originality even if the layout-design has later become common in the field.

1. H. Wager p. 99.
2. Patents Act §2: 'Patents may be granted only for inventions which are new in relation to what was known before the filing date of the patent application...'

580. A layout-design which is created through a combination of parts of a protected layout-design is protected according to the same principle as a collected work is in copyright law.

581. Paragraph 4 of the Act lays down certain criteria concerning the citizenship of the person who has created a layout-design or the person to whom the exclusive right has been transferred. The principal rule is that an exclusive right is held by a person who is a Finnish citizen or who is a permanent resident of Finland. The principle of reciprocity generally accepted by industrialised countries means that the citizens of countries with whom Finland has signed bilateral agreements or international conventions on the protection of layout-designs may also be granted an exclusive right to a layout-design in Finland.

§4. Formalities (Procedures for Grant and Obtaining Protection)

582. The exclusive right to a layout-design is obtained by registration (Sect. 3). The competent registration authority is the Patent Office (Sect. 13). The registration application must be made no later than two years from the day when the layout-design was first distributed to the public, for example, through sale. The country in which the first distribution took place is not relevant. Registration applications made after the said two year period cannot be approved.

583. The application must be made in writing and must contain all materials necessary to identify the layout-design. Further stipulations are contained in the Decree on the Exclusive Right to the Layout-Design of an Integrated Circuit (No. 946 of 1991). If some person other than the creator of the layout-design applies for registration, an explanation must be attached demonstrating the applicant's right to the layout-design. Registration of two or more layout-designs may not be sought in a single application (Sect. 15). This limitation makes the application clearer and easier to process. Foreign applicants must be represented by an agent based in Finland.

584. A fast and simple application procedure is used in the registration procedure.[1] This means that the registering authority only checks that the formal criteria for granting an exclusive right to a layout-design have been satisfied, i.e. that the matter concerns a layout-design according to Section 1, that it falls within the scope of the law according to Section 2 and has been filed within the time limit of two years according to Section 5.

1. Compare with the Finnish Utility Model Act (No. 800 of 1991).

585. During the processing of the application, another person may claim to have a greater right to the layout-design. The question of who has the greater right will ultimately be settled in court (through a civil action).[1] Any person or persons shown to have a greater right to a layout-design than the applicant may have the application for the registration of the layout-design in question transferred to them.

1. H. Wager pp. 101–102.

586. Approval of the registration is announced and entered in the Register of Layout-Designs (Sect. 22). Entry into the Register enjoys official reliability. Transfers of an exclusive right to a layout-design and mortgage rights must be entered in the Register. In situations where there has been a previous assignment to another person the first assignment has no effect on the second assignee if the second assignee acted in good faith at the time and registered the acquisition before the first assignee (Sect. 23).

§5. Ownership and Transfer (Assignment – Licences)

587. An exclusive right belongs to the person who created the layout-design or to the person to whom the right has been transferred. Only a natural person can create a layout-design (Sect. 3). However, the person who has created a layout-design is often in an employment relationship[1] to a legal person and, according to the principal rule, the employer has the right to register the layout-design provided that the employee has created the layout-design within the context of his normal job description. If a layout-design is created by a person working in the fields of research or education within a university, then the university has the right to register the layout-design only if this has been expressly agreed.

1. By an employment relationship is understood a relationship between an employer and an employee based on an employment contract in accordance with Sect. 1 of the Employment Contracts Act (No. 320 of 1970). In such an employment contract, the employee agrees to perform work for the employer under his direction and supervision in return for wages or other compensation. In such a relationship the employer has the right to obtain the exclusive right to a layout-design through registration if the layout-design was created while performing work assignments.

588. The right to a layout-design may also be transferred through normal transfers of property such as sale, gift, inheritance or bequest. If several persons have created a layout-design together, then the exclusive right is granted to the whole group collectively. The question of who is to receive the exclusive right may also be settled through agreement or, where no agreement has been reached, through the common principles of civil law.

589. Section 8 of the Act contains rules similar to those of intellectual property law concerning the right to transfer the right of use of a protected work by means of agreement (licencing). The right to use a layout-design may be transferred in whole or only in part. The transfer may also be exclusive, i.e. no person other than the licensee may use the object transferred. According to the principal rule, a transferred right may be further transferred. If a transferor wishes to limit the rights of a licensee to assign the licence, then such an express condition must be stated in the licencing agreement.

590. Section 39 concerns the right of a holder of an exclusive right to seek a court order preventing an imminent or ongoing infringement of the said right. According to subsection 39.3, for some special reason the court may grant permission for the protected layout-design to be distributed to the public or otherwise used in return for specific compensation. In practice this subsection is only used after negotiations between the parties have broken down. The application of the subsection results in a right similar to that of a compulsory licence, which is why the application of the subsection requires some special reason.

§6. Scope of Exclusive Rights

591. An exclusive right to a layout-design is obtained by registering the layout-design. The exclusive right means that the holder has the right to determine the use of the layout-design. The use of a registered layout-design requires the consent of the holder of the exclusive right. The exclusive right includes the right to produce, copy or distribute the protected layout-design to the public, e.g. by sale, rental or loan. A layout-design may also be distributed without a specimen being distributed *in concreto*, e.g. by sending a file through a data network. The exclusive right is limited only to distribution to the public. According to the Government Bill on the Act, the word 'public' refers to an unspecified number of natural or legal persons. The consent of the holder of the right to a layout-design must be secured in order to import it or otherwise bring it into the country.

592. Ownership of an instance of a protected layout-design and the exclusive right thereto are two different things. A person who purchases an integrated circuit does not, through the right of ownership, acquire the right to copy the layout-design. The right to copy the layout-design requires, with certain exceptions (*q.v.* Sect. 9), the agreement of the holder of the exclusive right.

§7. Limitations of the Scope of Protection

593. Although the Act presupposes that the person who has created the layout-design holds the exclusive right to it and that any use thereof requires the agreement of the holder of the exclusive right, there are certain exceptions to this main rule. According to Section 9, a copy of a protected layout-design may be made by anyone for private use, for teaching and for analysis. Private use is defined as copying for one's own personal use or for one's immediate circle such as family or close friends.

594. Copies made in order to perform a professional task or job of work are not covered by this exception. The concept 'education' includes both public and private as well as commercial education and education within an undertaking related to layout-designs. The analysis of a layout-design is understood to mean the disassembling of an integrated circuit in order to investigate how it is constructed and functions, how the components are placed, and matters related to the manufacturing technique and characteristics of the circuit which are central to research and development. Exceptions are, for example, applied to universities, colleges, research institutes and research divisions in enterprises.

595. Section 10 covers so-called reverse engineering. By this it is understood that the results gained from analysing a circuit may be used without the permission of the legal holder of the right to its layout-design. The section recognises that it is important to be able to utilise and develop existing know-how within the technology related to integrated circuits. The agreement of the holder of the right to the layout-design which has been analysed is not needed if a new original circuit layout-design is created on the basis of the result of the analysis. This exception does not, however, include the use of ideas, logic, technical principles, functional principles or the like which are part of the circuit. The degree of originality required to register a circuit layout-design is determined in the final instance by the court. The exclusive right of the holder of an analysed circuit layout-design has no right to a new circuit layout-design which has been created by using the result of the analysis. The exclusive right belongs to the creator of the new circuit layout-design.

596. The exclusive right to a circuit layout-design is further limited by Section 11, according to which a person who, acting in good faith, has acquired an illegally produced, protected circuit layout-design, is protected. The protection of having acted in good faith also applies to successors. Circuits which have been acquired in good faith may be distributed without impediment or be imported into the country as long as the person who is distributing or importing them acts in good faith, i.e. neither knows nor suspects that the circuits have been illegally produced. Compensation by the distributor or importer commences after the protection of good faith has ceased. The compensation must be reasonable with regard to the interests of both parties and to the circumstances.

§8. Duration of Protection

597. According to Section 6, the duration of the exclusive right is ten years counted from the date on which the application for registration was made. If the circuit layout-design was distributed before the application for registration, then the exclusive right takes effect from the date when the circuit layout-design was first distributed (no longer than two years before the application for registration, *see* Sect. 5). The period of protection ceases at the end of the tenth calendar year counted from the date on which it began. After the period of protection has expired, the circuit design-layout may be freely used without the consent of the holder of the right.

598. According to Section 12, an exclusive right is used when a protected circuit layout-design is distributed or imported. The paragraph means that an integrated circuit which is legally distributed on the market, i.e. with the agreement of the holder of the exclusive right or in accordance with Section 11, may be further distributed. The section only applies to entire, complete circuits.

599. After the application procedure has been noted, it may be observed that the Patent Office has registered circuit layout-designs which do not satisfy the requirements for registration. At any time during or after the registration period, anyone may petition for the cancellation of the registration. In order to avoid unfounded requests, the claimant must pay a fee to the Patent Office for the request to be considered. The holder of the registration must be heard before a decision on a possible cancellation is made. If the Patent Office finds that formal obstacles to registration exist, then the registration may be cancelled in whole or in part. A total cancellation applies *ex tunc*.

600. In addition to cancellation, the registration may cease as a result of an appeal for nullification. Section 2 requires that the registration of a circuit layout-design be original. When processing applications the registering officials merely verify that the formal requirements have been satisfied. The requirement of originality is not verified. Circuit layout-designs which are registered despite a lack of originality may be nullified in a court of law. An action may be filed by anyone and there is no statute of limitations in the Act (Sect. 30).

601. A registration may cease through the transfer of an exclusive right to another person who has demonstrated that he has a stronger right to a registered circuit layout-design. An action for a transfer must be filed within one year counted from the date on which the claimant became aware of the registration and within a maximum of three years if the registered holder of the exclusive right has acted in good faith. If the holder of the exclusive right has in good faith begun work or made substantial preparations to exploit the protected circuit layout-design, then the right to continue may be granted against reasonable compensation. This right of use may not be further transferred. The original holder of the right thus has a kind of compulsory licence.

602. The holder of a circuit layout-design may at any time freely relinquish his exclusive right. The circuit layout-design is then removed from the circuit layout-design register. If an attachment is pending, then the layout-design may not be removed from the register.

§9. INFRINGEMENT AND REMEDIES

603. A breach of the law on circuit layout-designs occurs when protected integrated circuits are produced, distributed to the public or imported without the consent of the holder of the right.

604. The penal provisions of the Act divide offences against the exclusive right to the layout-design of an integrated circuit into two categories according to the gravity of the offence: circuit layout-design crimes and circuit layout-design misdemeanours (Sect. 35). An offence is classified as a crime if the action is intended to cause significant damage to the holder of the right and the offence has been committed wilfully and for profit. Conviction for a circuit layout-design misdemeanour requires wilful or gross negligence.

605. A person who wilfully or through negligence distributes, copies or imports protected circuit layout-designs without the due consent is liable to pay compensa-

Chip Protection, Ch. 8

tion to the holder of the exclusive right. Reasonable compensation must be paid for an infringement. Compensation for the damages suffered by the holder of the right is paid for using the circuit layout-design. The Act also contains a clause (Sect. 39) which makes it possible for the holder of the right to prevent the infringement from continuing.

The court may, on a motion submitted by the holder of the right, decide that illegal integrated circuits are to be destroyed or altered or surrendered against payment to the holder of the exclusive right.

§10. Overlapping and Relation to Other Intellectual Property Laws

606. Copyright law protects computer programs. Formerly, individual circuits could receive protection with the support of copyright law or of clauses in the law on unfair trade practices.

Chapter 9. Trade Secrets/Confidential Information

§1. SOURCES – LEGISLATION

Bibliography:
Aaltonen, A., *'Sopimattomasta menettelystä elinkeinotoiminnassa'* [Unfair Trade Practices], Vammala 1985;
Bärlund, J., *'Korruptionsbrotten inom näringslivet'* [Corruption in Trade], Helsingfors 1990;
Bruun, N., *'Konkurrens- och sekretessklausuler i anställningsavtal'* [Competition and Secrecy Clauses in Contracts of Employment], NIR 1988, pp. 71–80;
Castrén, M., *'EU-Suomen markkinaoikeus'* [Market Law in EU-Finland], Helsinki 1997.
Rissanen, K. & Tiili, V. & Mäkinen, P., *'Markkinaoikeuden perusteet'* [Fundamentals of Market Law], Jyväskylä 1990;

Official documents and publications:
Unfair Trade Practices Act No. 1061 of 1978;
Government Bill No. 114 of 1978;
Penal Code Chapter 30;
Employment Contracts Act No. 320 of 1970.

§2. THE PROTECTION OF TRADE SECRETS/CONFIDENTIAL INFORMATION

607. Traditionally the concept of a trade secret or confidential information in commercial life has not been defined in Finnish legislation, although it has been used in many legal sources. When the Penal Code and its Chapter 30 were revised in 1990, an attempt was made to define this concept in legislation.[1] According to Chapter 30 Section 11 of the Penal Code, a trade secret is a business or professional secret or some such corresponding information concerning a certain trade or business which the trader keeps confidential and the disclosure of which could cause economic damage either to his trade or to another trader who disclosed the information to him. A description of a trade secret was already included in the 1978 Government Bill for the Unfair Trade Practices Act. Here a trade secret was described as a circumstance the confidentiality of which is important to the business or trade of the enterprise possessing the knowledge of it.

1. Concerning the revision of Chapter 30 of the Penal Code, *see* J. Bärlund pp. 67*ff*.

608. Basically, a trade secret consists of information. The information may be saved in a document, as a prototype, on a computer or in someone's head (i.e. in memory). A trade secret may concern different parts of a business. Economic secrets may concern contract relations, production issues or marketing (pricing policies, granting of discounts), budgets or offers. Technical trade secrets are those

Trade Secrets/Confidential Information, Ch. 9

relating to structures, materials and transport as well as to manufacturing, product development and know-how. Some secrets concern the organisation while others concern the strategies and policies of an enterprise. All of the above may influence the competitive position of the enterprise.[1]

1. M. Castrén pp. 267–268.

609. A condition for the existence of a trade secret is a legitimate interest of the possessor/trader to keep the information confidential. This means that the confidential information is important for the enterprise when considering its position in relation to its competitors or potential competitors. If the information is disclosed, this may harm/damage the enterprise. There is not, however, any requirement that the information should be explicitly classified as confidential in any respect or that the importance of confidentiality should have been stressed to, for example, the employees. If the information becomes public due to inadequate protection, then it is no longer a trade secret.[1]

1. K. Rissanen, V. Tiili & P. Mäkinen p. 242.

610. The most important rules on trade secrets are to be found in the Unfair Trade Practices Act Section 4, paragraphs 1 and 2. Here it is stipulated that no one may, without justification, obtain or attempt to obtain information regarding a trade secret or to use or disclose any information thus obtained. Furthermore, no employee of a trader, who has obtained information regarding a trade secret may, while being employed, without justification disclose it in order to obtain a benefit for himself or for a third party or to injure the interests of another.[1]

1. A. Aaltonen pp. 150*ff.*

611. In Section 4, paragraphs 3 and 4 it is stipulated that no one who, while performing an act on behalf of a trader, has obtained information regarding a trade secret or who, for the purpose of performing a task related to the trade, has been entrusted with a technical model or technical instruction, may use or disclose it without justification. No one who has obtained information regarding a trade secret, technical model or technical instruction from another, knowing that the said person has obtained or disclosed information without justification, may use or disclose the information in question.

612. A trader who has used or disclosed a trade secret, technical model or technical instruction of another in violation of the provisions of Section 4 may be enjoined from continuing or repeating the said practice. The injunction is to be reinforced with the threat of a fine unless, for special reasons, this is deemed unnecessary. This injunction is issued by a specialist court, the Market Court, which decides cases arising under the Unfair Trade Practices Act as well as cases pertaining to consumer protection.[1]

1. K. Rissanen, V. Tiili & P. Mäkinen p. 196.

613. Sections 15 and 16 of the Employment Contracts Act also include restrictions on the use of confidential information obtained during employment. These restrictions rarely continue after the employment relationship has ended, although there might be some contractual arrangements which seek to ensure this (*see* Sect. 16a).[1]

1. N. Bruun p. 72.

614. Industrial espionage is criminalised in Chapter 30 Section 4 of the Penal Code. No one may, without justification, obtain or try to obtain information concerning a trade secret. Actual use or disclosure of the information is therefore not required.

615. A person who commits industrial espionage may be punished only if the intentional act satisfies the essential elements of Chapter 30 Section 4 of the Penal Code concerning the ways in which the person has obtained or tried to obtain information. The exhaustive list is given in this section of the Penal Code.[1]

1. K. Rissanen, V. Tiili & P. Mäkinen p. 244.

616. Chapter 30, Section 5, paragraph 1, point 1 of the Penal Code concerns betrayal of trust. A person who, while in an employment relationship, has received information about a trade secret must not unlawfully use or disclose the secret during his term of service in order to secure economic benefits for himself or another or to harm a third party. The restrictions regarding disclosure are strict during an employment relationship. Points 2–4 of this paragraph concern persons other than employees. According to these subsections, persons who unlawfully, in order to secure economic/financial benefits for themselves or others, disclose a trade secret or use a trade secret thus obtained:

– while serving as a member of the board of governors of an association, or foundation, as a managing director, an auditor or receiver or in a comparable position,
– while performing a task on behalf of another or otherwise in a confidential business relationship, or
– in connection with the reorganisation of an enterprise

may be punished for disclosing a trade secret.

617. The restrictions of these persons continue even after the performance of the tasks referred to. This is quite natural when considering the often quite independent status of the managing director as well as the confidential information obtained when functioning as an outsider on commission, e.g. as a lawyer, a consultant, an engineer or an advertising agency. The commission may be of short duration and important business secrets may be conferred so that it is necessary that the confidentiality obligation is absolute and that it is not limited to the period of the performance of the commission.[1]

1. N. Bruun p. 73.

618. Legal proceedings concerning criminal offences and the application of the Penal Code are tried in the general courts and may proceed from the District Court to the Court of Appeal and further to the Supreme Court. The Market Court, on the other hand, is the sole instance for cases arising under the Unfair Trade Practices Act.

619. There is an extensive body of case law concerning trade secrets. Most cases deal with the obligations of employees and their behaviour in handling various kinds of confidential information.

Index

The numbers given refer to paragraph numbers.

Absolute product protection: 281
Act of the Rights to Employee Inventions: 264
Act on Breeder's Rights: 339
Act on Damages: 193
Act on the Exclusive Right to the Layout-Design of an Integrated Circuit: 38, 576
Act on Restriction of Competition: 272
Adaption rights: 115–118
Agricultural products: 538
Application fee: 250
Application procedure: 347
Architecture,
 – products of: 24, 27, 52, 91, 110, 121, 132, 136
Artistic handicrafts and industrial arts: 24, 28, 53, 91, 110, 121, 132
Artistic works: 20–21, 24, 44, 389, 515
Association marks: 368
Audio-visual works: 32
Auditor: 616
Auxiliary trade name: 487–488

Bankruptcy: 78, 174, 271, 420, 520–521
Berne Convention: 12, 18, 43, 129
Betrayal of trust: 616
Blank tape levy: 126, 139
Board of Business Practice of the Central Chamber of Commerce: 481
Breeder's exemption: 561
Budapest Treaty: 247

Certificate of Home State: 405
Cinematographic works: 24, 31–32, 54–55, 62, 86, 110, 125, 132, 139, 154, 165

Circuit layout-design crime: 604
Circuit layout-design misdemeanour: 604
Claim: 235–244, 252, 286, 553, 583
Classic work: 93, 100–101
Collecting societies: 83–89, 92, 123, 126–127, 178–179
Collective marks: 357, 368
Collective Marks Act: 357, 368, 371
Combination inventions: 232
Combined marks: 364
Commercial exploitation: 274–275, 346, 537, 541, 558, 563
Commissioned works: 70
Community exhaustion: 134–135, 177, 181–182, 290, 292
Community Plant Variety Authority: 538
Community Trademark Office: 412
Community Trademark: 389, 404, 412
Community Trademark Regulation: 355
Comparative advertising: 444
Comparative marketing: 444, 480
Compensation: 126, 191–192, 324, 330–332, 334–336, 352, 467, 569, 590, 596, 601, 605
Competent court: 325, 473
Compilation works: 32, 34, 36, 39, 41, 57, 62, 90
Compulsory licences: 84, 89–92, 127, 157, 292, 302–309, 351, 528, 557, 590, 601
Computer Program Directive: 134, 140
Computer programs: 31, 39–40, 55, 59, 68, 95, 99, 110, 125, 132, 134, 136, 140–143, 184, 198, 207, 214, 606
Computer software: 39–40
Concert programs: 155

165

Index

Confidentiality: 199, 341
Contractual licences: 83–88, 127
Contributory infringement: 278, 285
Control marks: 368
Convention priority: 226
Copyright Act: 15–17, 19–21, 35, 40, 44, 79, 83, 89, 93, 99, 102, 105, 120, 130, 164, 174, 185, 188–190, 502
Copyright Council: 19, 25
Copyright Decree: 19, 159
Copyright misdemeanour: 190
Copyright offence: 189
Corporate invention: 260, 266
Corporate signs: 369–373
Counterclaim: 551–552
Counterfeiting: 482
Court of Arbitration: 270
Crown copyright: 36
Culpability,
 – degree of: 192, 332, 467
Current topics and events: 147–148
Customs Act: 482

Damages: 188–189, 191, 193, 328–331, 334–335, 373, 466–467, 469, 472, 497, 501, 566, 569, 604–605, 607, 609
Database Directive: 42, 183
Databases: 41–42, 55, 140–144, 183–184, 199
Declatory judgment: 337, 568
Decompilation,
 – of a program: 143
Decree on the Exclusive Right to the Layout-Design of an Integrated Circuit: 583
Decree on Plant Genera and Species: 543
Defensive mark: 424
Degenerate: 460–461
Dependent patents: 306
Description: 245–247, 547
Descriptive mark: 379, 383, 385
Direct infringement: 278
Discovery: 205–207
Distinctive, Distinctiveness: 361–362, 365, 374–375, 377–383, 385, 398, 400, 403, 407, 430, 433, 436, 457–460
Distraint: 77–78, 174, 420
Division and reparation: 257

Double protection: 537
Droit d'accès: 93, 102–103
Droit de modifier: 94
Droit moral: 93
Droit à la paternité: 93, 95–96
Droit de repentir: 94
Droit au respect: 93, 97
Droit de retrait: 94
Droit de suite: 120–124, 171–172
Duration of protection,
 – chip protection: 597–602
 – copyright: 164–173
 – industrial design: 529–530
 – patent: 311–326
 – plant variety: 564–567
 – trademark: 455–464

Economic rights: 64, 72–74, 94, 102–104, 167, 523
Economic secret: 608
Employee inventions: 264–270
Employee Inventions Board: 270
Employment Contracts Act: 613
Equivalence: 287
Establishment: 358, 360–361, 365, 368, 371, 374, 393–400, 413, 415, 417, 425, 433, 442, 484, 487–488, 493
European Economic Area (EEA): 124, 134, 168, 181–182, 185, 290–292, 438–440, 524
European Patent Convention (EPC): 202, 229, 279, 313, 321, 326, 538
European Patent Organisation (EPO): 212, 229
Evident abuse: 228
Ex nunc: 324
Ex tunc: 324, 599
Examination: 546, 553
Examination of requirements: 251–252
Execution: 271
Exhaustion,
 – of copyright: 131–135
 – of an industrial design: 524
 – of a patent: 290–292
 – of a trademark: 438–440
Exhibit the work,
 – right to: 114

Index

Experiments: 294
Exploitation rights: 104–126
Expropriation: 271, 310

Farmer's privilege: 561
Figure marks: 363
Film: 181
Fine: 189–190, 352, 470, 572
Finnish Broadcasting Company: 92
First-to-file: 223, 262
Flag: 387, 515
Force majeure: 453
Formalities,
 – chip protection: 582–586
 – industrial design: 516–518
 – plant variety: 546–554
 – patent protection: 234–259
 – trademarks: 400–415
Future works: 75

Hybrid: 563

Impediment,
 – absolute: 386–388
 – to registration: 386–392, 515, 545, 568, 596
 – relative: 389–392
Implied agreement: 64, 72
Indirect product protection: 278, 282
Industrial application,
 – capability of: 204, 215
Industrial espionage: 298, 614–615
Industrial property offence: 329
Industrial rights offence: 470
Infringement: 188–195, 281, 297, 300, 327–337, 340, 349, 352, 389, 465–473, 501, 530–532, 568–573, 590, 603–605
Initial authorship: 55, 75
Injunction: 612
Innovation charge: 534
Integrated circuits: 38, 200, 574–578, 592, 594–595, 598, 603–605
Interface: 143
Interim injunction: 473
Interim protection: 571
Interlocutory injunction: 328
International applicability: 284

International Convention for the Protection of New Varieties of Plants: 537
International exhibition: 228
International traffic: 301
Invalidity: 323, 336, 457
Invention: 204–214, 236, 238–242, 245–248, 257, 261–263, 265–269
Inventive step: 216, 218, 222, 224, 229–233, 242, 252, 281, 344–345, 347–348, 513

Joint authorship: 95
Joint ownership: 225
Joint proprietorship: 59–60, 97, 165, 263
Joint works: 59–62

Kodak doctrine: 434, 496

Licences: 79–82, 272–273, 351, 421, 521, 556–557, 566, 589
Literary works: 20–23, 27, 39, 41, 44, 50, 59, 90, 117, 156, 160, 175–176, 195–197, 389, 515
Logo: 364

Madrid Protocol: 355, 411
Mandatory provision: 269
Manufacture,
 – place of: 384
Market Court: 373, 481, 612, 618
Marketing campaign: 394
Markings on goods: 289
Ministry of Agriculture and Forestry: 535, 546, 555
Ministry of Trade and Industry: 13
Minor patent: 345
Misleading: 462
Moral rights: 73, 93–103, 130, 177
Mortgage: 72, 271, 273, 420, 586
Multiple registration: 518
Mutatis mutandis: 358, 368, 493

National Board of Patents and Registration (NBPR): 13, 203, 234, 356, 401, 410–412, 432, 488, 516–517, 529, 573
National Survey Board: 66
Neighbouring rights: 134–135, 174–189

Index

Non-commercial use: 293, 346
Non-working patent: 305
Novelty: 218–223,
   – exceptions of: 224–228, 252

Obligatory provision: 266
OECD: 537
Opposition: 255
Opposition submission: 409
Original work: 35
Overall assessment: 288
Ownership, and transfer of: 55–57, 260–263, 271, 416–421, 519–521, 551–552, 555–557, 587–590, 592

Parallel importation: 292, 439–440
Parallel trade name: 487
Paris Convention: 11, 201, 301, 343, 354, 404, 452, 484, 503
Passivity-rule: 446
Patent agent: 234, 251
Patent Agents Act: 234
Patent Co-operation Treaty (PCT): 202
Patent Office: 13, 203, 215, 222–223, 234–235, 243, 249, 251–256, 260, 270, 286, 313, 316, 318, 320–322, 325, 345–346, 348, 426, 488, 582, 599
Patent Regulations: 203
Patents Act: 201–204, 229, 279, 283, 290, 303, 312, 323, 329, 335, 339, 511–513, 524, 528, 530, 568-569, 573, 579
Patents Decree: 201, 203, 236, 238, 240, 244, 247-249, 257, 312
Penal Code: 189, 327, 329, 470, 607, 615–616, 618
Penal sanctions: 189
Performing artists,
   – rights of: 144, 175–179
Performing rights: 111–114
Person skilled in the art: 216–217, 222, 230, 232, 245, 281, 287–288, 321
Phonograph record: 178–180
Photocopying: 84, 106
Photographic works and pictures: 29–30, 51, 121
Photographs: 117, 144, 151, 185–186

Pictoral art,
   – works of: 26, 51
Piracy: 189, 192
Plant Variety Board: 546
Plant Variety Protection Act: 536, 540, 546, 551, 558, 561, 568, 572
Preclusion-rule: 423, 445
Press reports: 187
Prior use,
   – right of: 296–300, 526
Priority,
   – to enjoy: 249
Priority in time: 552
Private use,
   – reproduction for: 131, 136–139, 163, 184, 525, 593
Procedural Code: 328, 466
Process patent: 209, 214, 282–283
Process protection: 278
Producers' rights: 62, 144, 180–181
Product patent: 208–209, 280
Product protection: 278
Protection,
   – the scope of:
      – industrial design: 524–528
      – integrated circuits: 593–596
      – patents: 286–288
      – plant variety: 561–563
      – trademarks: 438–448
      – trade names: 495–498
      – utility models: 344–352
Public announcement: 551
Public authorities: 36–37
Public interest: 307
Public lending right: 125
Public performance,
   – right to: 111–113, 154
Public statements and documents: 149–150
Publicity,
   – of documents: 258–259

Quotation: 144–146

Radio and television transmissions: 84, 86, 92, 144, 148, 157–158, 161–163, 177–179, 182

Index

Rat poison doctrine: 496
Receiver: 616
Reciprocity,
- the principle of: 581
Register of Layout-Designs: 586
Registered designs: 197
Registered Designs Act: 49, 475, 502, 506, 508, 523–524
Registered Designs Decree: 512, 518
Remedies: 188–194, 327–337, 465–473, 501, 530–531, 568–573, 603–605
Remuneration: 17, 88–89, 91, 120–125, 127, 154, 178–179, 264, 266, 269
Rental Directive: 91, 134
Replicability: 217
Reproduction: 156–160
Reproduction rights: 106
Reverse engineering: 141, 294, 595
Revocation: 321, 336, 459
Royalty: 82

Satellite Broadcasting Directive: 86
Secondary mark: 488, 493
Secondary meaning: 385
Secondary trade name: 487
Secondary work: 35
Seize: 327–328
Semiconductors: 577–578
Simultaneous retransmission: 87
Spare parts: 301, 443, 476, 506, 518
Succession: 76
Suggestive marks: 383
Sui generis right: 183
Supplementary protection certificates,
- for medicinal products: 312
- for protection products: 315
Symbol: 358, 360, 363, 365, 368–373, 387, 389, 391, 393, 395–399, 413, 422–423, 434, 436, 441, 443, 456, 471–472, 477, 479, 515

Target group: 395–396, 398, 427–429, 433–436
Technical effect: 216
Technical secret: 608

Telle quelle: 406
Temporary injunction: 466
Termination: 320, 457
Title, pseudonym, signature: 33, 58
Tort Liability: 193
Trade Names Act: 371, 478, 483, 485–486, 489, 491, 494, 500–501
Trade Register Act: 485, 488, 491
Trade secret: 341, 607–614, 616, 619
Trademark agent: 401
Trademarks Act: 353, 355–357, 365, 368, 371–372, 416, 421, 435, 438, 457, 465, 473, 477, 482, 568
Trademarks Decree: 356
Trademarks Directive: 355, 362, 365, 435, 438
Transfer: 72–78, 416–421, 500, 589, 601
Transistor: 578
Transition period: 172–173
Transition provisions: 168–173
Translation rights: 119
Travaux préparatoires: 44–45, 70, 134, 170
Treaty of Rome: 272
TRIPS Agreement: 168, 202, 283, 538–539

Unfair Competition Act: 502
Unfair Trade Practices Act: 199, 289, 340, 373, 441, 444, 479, 607, 610, 612, 618
UPOV conventions: 339, 536–538, 541, 548–549, 555
Use patent: 209
Use requirements: 449–454
Utility Model Act: 338, 342, 344, 348–349
Utility Model Decree: 342

Variety name: 547
Vegetative Propagation: 560
Violation of a patent right: 329

Washington Convention (of the WIPO): 576
Word marks: 361
Works made for hire: 63–71
World Intellectual Property Organisation (WIPO): 12, 576–577
Worl d Trade Organisation: 403

Index